GOD'S MANIFESTATION OF THE HEART

God's Manifestation of The Heart

Enhance your knowledge with the insight of who God is

Advantage
BOOKS

Robin (Rochel) Arne

God's Manifestation of the Heart by Robin (Rochel) Arne
Copyright © 2022 by Robin Arne
All Rights Reserved.
ISBN: 978-1-59755-689-7

Published by: ADVANTAGE BOOKS™, Longwood, FL, www.advbookstore.com

Unless otherwise indicated, Scriptures marked NIV are taken from the NEW INTERNATIONAL VERSION (NIV): Scripture taken from THE HOLY BIBLE, NEW INTERNATIONAL VERSION ®. Copyright© 1973, 1978, 1984, 2011 by Biblica, Inc.TM. Used by permission of Zondervan

Library of Congress Catalog Number: 22022939796

Editor: Roxy Heinrichs

First Printing: July 2022
22 23 24 25 26 27   10 9 8 7 6 5 4 3 2 1

Acknowledgements

My desire is to include the people I love as my inspiration. There have been many. My father, who is always the social butterfly, instructs fellowship. My mother always encourages all I do, and she enables me to express myself freely. My daughter is a gifted woman of hope who, herself, can write with beauty. My son showers me with wisdom in the form of strength and endurance that I see him put forth in his life daily. My sister grants me her time with phone calls of in-depth messages of the heart where no judgement is placed against me. And finally, my Savior, who always leads my pen strokes and divulges truth to my heart in such a way that I hear unity in His voice.

These people have all entertained me personally in their home and I have been invited in with love and adoration. These are gifts of the spirit that grace and shower one with hope. I never feel alone in their presence. I love each of these individually, and they are treasured.

God's Manifestations of The Heart ...

Is a workbook offering the reader a chance to read a passage of insight then witness the recorded thoughts of the author who has engaged with God, and understood His message therein. Spacing has been drafted for you as the reader to record your own thoughts and insights you have gleaned, and to reflect on what the message means to you personally. In doing so you will find a fulfillment that has grafted you closer to God Himself.

I highly encourage you to read the Bible each day and learn directly from God all His truths. His Word is complete. I am a mere person who engages and trusts His leadership. He has never failed me, and He won't fail you either.

God's flower of forgiveness has petals of truth that never fade. Bathe in its beauty and know peace like a river where divine inspiration and understanding nurture the ground where it lives.

Growing in wisdom is found by the vibrations of God's heart to yours from reading what He has in store in His Bible. When finding truth, a heart always clings to what God has spoken of in His Word. It is true and honorable, and there is never cause for alarm. God's grace is on every page. Each trinket is of silver quality that surpasses the highest standard. The gold standard surpasses even the slightest admission of truth concerning whom to trust each day. God is that jewel. He is the one you can always rely on. He never fails and He shows favoritism to none. You can take His words as Gospel, and you won't be deceived even in the slightest of ways. God is purity, and His character is solid. He grafts with wisdom, and He places a knitted garment around the heart to keep it safe and secure with purpose and a forthright perspective so as to lead with clarity. God holds all of man close. Even when doubt is present, He continues to engage and secure a position with Him if Christ is the one you have chosen to follow.

A green leaf is green because God has blown color into it.

Color is grafted by the hand of God. It is a characteristic of His beauty to our eyes. He is color and hue that we don't understand. He can be the sun, moon and stars yet hold the color white at bay on a bridge of purity in the mind.

One never doubts God's authority when he takes on a challenge that only God can provide answers to. He reigns supreme in all He does. This is proven true when one watches over a group of children. You can see the glimmer of hope each face holds, and it represents a style unique to the King Jesus. Only He can grant a display of beauty where teeth meet the lips, and a union produces joy. God does this with ease, and He graces our hearts in the same way. Trust God and be delivered into freedom where hope prevails and causes the wind to dissipate away from the just cause of Christ.

You can find your mission in life by choosing first a path of the living Word. It will guide your steps and teach you a story all at the same time. There is much to learn in the Word of God, and you will find peace there always.

_____

_____

_____

_____

_____

_____

_____

_____

_____

_____

_____

_____

_____

_____

_____

A fountain is splashing only when God provides the water, and a balance of wet perfume to dampen the skin and refresh the heart.

God is the center and the time clock. He travels the world and knows the heart of every man. He works in favor of each person and totes their health as a magistrate of individuality in the form of growth toward His person. No one shall ever be enlightened to the point of knowing the whole of God. He is too vast and knowledgeable. Man is small in comparison, and he sees with eyes of doubt and disdain. God on the other hand sees with clarity, and He knows the volume of each syllable that enters every heart. This is truth and order at its finest. Look to Christ for each detail you need to understand. He is the one who will transform your spirit and guide you with hope to conquer every battle that comes your way.

Even a clown knows the bull is but a beast that can be led with a bridle should he be tamed with grain. God operates differently. He crafts with care, and a plate of purity where we dine on a delight that inspires the gifts of the spirit into submission in which a total desire for God takes place. This is the connection that leads one on a mission of growth where a union of the mind embraces God's hold on the heart. You see clearly and gain wisdom when the tidal wave leaves the beach. In this way God's spirit acknowledges those who listen and seek wise counsel from His book, the Bible. You can't go wrong when you read the contents therein.

_____

_____

_____

_____

_____

_____

_____

_____

_____

_____

_____

_____

A triple dose of hope is found when God is the factor of study.

Grass the color green is a benefactor bestowed by the hand of the Almighty. Even this is a simple feat for Him to master. If you think you are alone, remember God can hear every thought, and He knows every action of the heart. God witnesses a time and place, and calls it His own because He crafts in the form of love, to each person, an understanding where hope lives.

God never leaves anyone in the dust. He carries them into the light, and they realize their mission is solid and true once they accept the call God put forth. Locate a path and look where it leads. Is it a place of purity with a boundless given mentality of divine inspiration? Can you feel the heartbeat of the Lord as you think on its perspective to others? Are you granted favor in the form of understanding that surpasses a dark initiative otherwise seen from above as a lost cause? Can you expect good things to come your way because you have chosen wisely? Can you hear rewards on the platter of truth resting secure in your mind? If these things are true, you are on the right path with God leading your steps. If you hear nothing but blank opportunities with no ground to support the work you are doing then turn away and seek wise counsel as to free your spirit from deception, and the deceit of lies will diminish.

Once you shut out the dark, light will settle in and replace an empty depravity with a solid gold initiative that leads to beauty and charm of the heart. You can hear the spirit of the Lord when you engage with His person in prayer. It is a simple act that leads to many rewards. Knowing God brings a peace and harmony that only believers can relate to. Try today to stand strong in the faith. You will grow and flourish in the direction of goodness and mercy. You will overflow with divine understanding, and there will be a glow of righteousness that is seen by others. Each of these is worth more than gold.

Traveling across the countryside brings the eye different views, but the Word of the Lord brings truth and an experience denied by none.

A person is fast when they run amuck around the planet in doubt or disillusion. The fact no one ever understands how to manage their thoughts to a balance of integrity is not a question understood or heard unless God directs the steps and leads the person with grace. Planting and harvesting are fruitful when the seasons hold good weather. God is the one who harvests a pattern of good hope within the heart, and He grazes the pastures of righteousness if He hears a call to His name. Anyone can be a part of ministry if they trust the lead God offers or plants within them. He will make a way for growth to take place. He is good that way.

_____

_____

_____

_____

_____

_____

_____

_____

_____

_____

_____

_____

_____

_____

_____

_____

_____

Glowing reviews from an author of insight, gifts one with pride, however, a brush of death awakens the spirit into expectation that there is a God. The latter is more prosperous to the soul and mind.

Teaching others to understand a problem can be difficult when things are hidden in meaning. God's Word is a blanket of understanding free to all who choose His path of righteousness. Taking the step forward to know God is a plan of integrity. The more you relate to the Lord the more He speaks to you His grace and love. God is a Father. He is someone who favors the people He created. He does not leave them to fend for themselves. He carries them over all trial and ground of turbulence. God the creator will never leave you or forsake you. It is not His way to be distant or aloof. God loves and He cares for all man. Even the ones who step away from His good way. Those are the ones He longs to know better. A heart of doubt can be lifted, and carried to hope with a simple step toward the King Jesus. Simply express your faith in His person, and be refreshed in the knowledge that God is real. He will honor you when you do this in an act of faith. Never doubt God can hear your thoughts. You can't deny Him in your heart but mouth the words of acceptance. He will know true commitment in spite of any deception. You can know God personally by praying and reading His Word, the Bible. These two are gifts to His spirit. Engage with Him and receive a balance unknown to man in any other form. You will be rich with knowledge when you do.

_____

_____

_____

_____

_____

_____

_____

_____

_____

_____

_____

_____

Grafting a title page grants the expectation that a book will come into view once a story has been told. The Bible has many authors, and each book within is priceless with abundant hope.

An intellect that holds the character God as a statue of importance does not understand the King Jesus at all. Our God, the father, is a Master and a find of excellence. All the unity God offers to His people, as to His character and make up, is calibrated by His hand and heart. He never doubts or loses control, and in His person stands a creation that is complete. Nothing else compares and there is none who can build such a magnitude of favor like God is able to. Grafting to His heart will deploy a standard of hope that gifts you in such a way that you are lifted into the light and clarity prevails in your thought process. Every time you enact a dream you have begun a plan God has placed within you, and He will lead you along day by day with focus and a plan before you. Trust the direction God leads, and you will feel peace with a dash of excitement knowing you are in His will. This pleases the heart, and brings it joy beyond measure. Accept what you know as truth from God above and glide along as if connected to a cloud. God can do this for you and He will. You need only listen to His leadership through the Word He has prepared. It will grant you wisdom, and knowledge will come as a result of your faithfulness in scriptures. Understanding is a guidance where man engages with the spirit of God, and He instructs that person with a delivered meaning of greatness true to His character of purity. If you feel led to sin realize God is not the one you are following. You have been led astray. Let light be your guidance and embrace the goodness that follows. You will be enhanced and share a spirit with the King Jesus. His salvation to you is real. Accept it and glean righteousness on a daily walk through the kingdom of truth found at the foot of the cross. Jesus rests there, true and secure with good measure pressed down, shaken and restored with faith. No one comes to the Father but through Him.

The witness of a person is sand amongst the masses that rubs the heart raw and teaches each person truth and understanding when it lands in his heart.

God's power is true, and it centers a soul in the right way. You can feel the strength of a witness when truth is told. No single person can carry the load of telling all there is to know concerning how to know each detail of the Word of God. That is why we are told to read the Word of the Bible for ourselves, and let God do His work within our spirits. A manifestation takes place, and we learn how to understand the writings and their content becomes clear. It takes practice and a patience with a commitment that leads to clarity. One should look at learning who God is as a test of faith that needs fuel to thrive. Without it we are lost and struggling with no guidance. You can find hope within the Word of God, and you will learn how to deal with all your daily struggles as well as rejoice in the crafting God has put forth which is a token of His greatness designed with us in mind. Reading the Word makes a statement that you love and honor the true King of the world, Jesus Christ. He is faithful and full of love and devotion to all His people. That is you as well as me. We are set apart for the knowledge He offered was grasped and landed securely within us. It makes us part of His family, the bride. A wedding is coming in which we will partake and be at peace forever more. This wedding secures our place in heaven with the Father because Jesus chose to die for our sins. No other offers such a great sacrifice. Learn to understand this important find. You will do well to remember the great lengths the Son embarked upon for His glory and for our good. There is nothing greater to realize than this one true piece of gold that holds the key to all mankind.

_____

_____

_____

_____

_____

_____

_____

_____

_____

_____

_____

The event you hold on to is one that your memory takes and binds to your heart. If you are tied to Christ your outlook is solid and true, for He is the ultimate being.

Giving the love you hold to another brings growth and hope in the form of commitment that binds then creates a unity. All God offers is of a nature that is true. No exceptions are made in this area of study. We learn by being available to listen to the instruction God offers and accepting it as truth. No one other than God can be all things at the same time. That is, He knows all and is committed to truth. Even a simple white lie can cause heartache. God does not deliver a lie in any form. He is solid and true to the core. Look at how much He did for His people in Israel so many years before Christ was born. Even then He was faithful and honest. He invested in this people group as He was their God. Through the years they failed at staying committed, but God never does. He does not faulter or misstep. He never propagates trouble or misfortune. He will, however, build a shadow and hide growth if people are against Him. He will cover the veil of knowledge with a cloud, and you won't see where to turn. This is how He guides and directs steps, so people understand where to turn in their walk with Him. Isn't that a purposeful God? Isn't that a clever way to instruct without harm or false dreams? Growing in faith is produced when one reads the Word of God in His Bible, and he prays on a constant basis. These qualities bring about a plan and its goal from God above. There is never doubt if you see clearly the steps before you, and you understand how to step each one in the form of unity that glorifies the Father. This is how you will engage in truth. When you follow this perspective, you will be blessed and know you are on the right track. This is how God works. Continue in faith and be blessed. This is how one gains entry into knowledge, and truth is laid bare. You can't go wrong when God is your King and Master. He is a delight to know. Gain His trust and you will go far.

Taking a look at yourself in the mirror is good practice in which you will know if a hair is out of place. In doing this practice with the heart you recognize when you are in trouble and need the Lord to act on your behalf. Hindsight is 20/20.

Regretting the past is a simple feat of the mind, but true repentance comes when one invites the Lord in as a witness to the wrongdoing. Next comes the forgiveness of sins. In this simple act of love, you can become a member of the bride of Christ. He welcomes all who come to him with a clear conscience in which He is the focus and the redeemer. No one knows the Father but through Christ alone. There is no other way to be saved. The cross is a statement of true identity. It teaches the man who is willing to understand all there is to know about redemption. Even a weak individual can recognize the one true Savior of the world is God and man in one. Jesus came to redeem the sinner not to abolish him from the face of the earth. He desires all of man to know Him personally, and to build a relationship with His person. Knowing the Lord is a simple feat. One need only to pray with an earnest heart and accept Him as the one true God. Everyone is welcome to know Jesus. He does not exclude anyone on race or color or heritage. All faiths do not lead to salvation. Only Knowing Jesus gains one entry to heaven. It is a fact that will not be denied. Anyone saying another Gospel is false teaching. You can gain knowledge by following the Word of the Lord written thousands of years ago. All the words are still true and apply to all people even in this day and age. Looking outside of scripture leads one down a path of lies, so step forward into truth and believe only on the God of Abraham, Isaac, and Jacob as recorded in the Word of God, His Bible. You can have truth and knowledge with this simple act of obedience. Teach others while you learn and gift them with hope as well. This is what a man of God does for his fellow mankind. It is a witness that brings forth love and growth toward God and His greatness. Decide today to be that person and know recognition of being a child of God. Today God calls all man. Answer Him and receive a justified life of purpose and opportunity at the hand of God and His mercy. Grace will abound and you will be set free.

_____

_____

_____

_____

_____

_____

_____

_____

_____

Every little bit of truth one gains is granted by the King Jesus and His Father. The two are one and tied for all eternity. This is a grand understanding that can't be understood without accepting the message of the cross. Know this and learn who God is through His Son.

Each person must search for truth with his own heart and mind. No one gets a free pass to learn about God unless they apply themselves spiritually. You can find truth when you seek to know His person by way of reading His Word and praying. All other steps are futile. They lead nowhere not even to heaven's gate or the promise therein. Always trusting another's dream will not give you peace or understanding, it will only confuse the issue at hand. Look to the Savior and know how to find truth by implementing your heart His direction. There is much you will learn if you do this practice regularly. Intervals of time spent with the King will bring you closer to His person and insight will follow. A plan will develop, and you will hear His voice speak to your heart. You will be guided into understanding with opportunity to grow on the forefront of all you do. Take what you have learned about life and transform this knowledge into an aspect of knowing the past holds nothing but lost time. Look to the future and you will gain unity in the form of spiritual guidance where all you do is real and just. Knowing God brings this about in the form of grace with love attached to its core center. How can this be? It is a design God implemented for man to know His person and to be saved. Let this guide you and set your thought pattern on the course of justice with God at the helm. You can do it with a simple profession and a genuine intent with no reservations. Even if you have doubt, take the step forward and gain entry to truth and a life of unity with grace abounding toward Jesus Himself. He will take the lead and you will know who to serve. Your spirit will rejoice as it will recognize who to trust. His Lordship is real, which all men recognize when they find this to be true. There is nothing holding you back but pride and fear. Both of these are not of God. They are deception from the enemy and the heart that has sin nature. All of this will lose its ground at the voice of truth professing faith in Christ. Gain salvation, it is a free gift with no strings attached, just faith in true form and a genuine heart.

_____

_____

_____

_____

_____

_____

_____

_____

All the people of the world belong in the arms of God. That was His plan from the start. You can gaze on His goodness wherever you look. The trees and the mountains declare His name in their beauty.

Knowing the Lord is a task that is not difficult or hard to endeavor upon. You can find Him in all you do whether it be a work of joy or a toil of hard labor, He is always there. He will encourage your steps when you trust His direction and guidance. You won't find a better partner or someone more worthy. God is not one to tarry when a work is underway. He is a guidance tool that makes a grand example of truth hidden in plain sight. Understanding the steps God has in mind is not difficult. Simply look at scripture to know when you are walking in truth or have been led astray by the enemy. God will never teach someone to sin or to do evil things. Greed is not of God nor is a contemplation of darkness in any form. God is always light and good influence is His way. Talk to Him daily and learn His will by reading the Word He put in His book the Bible. If you question the work you are doing perhaps it is your heart telling you to look with clear eyes as to the purpose for your labor. What is your motive? Do you desire to walk in faith and be led in clarity? Do you desire a wholesome avenue for your walk? Are you hoping for riches that aren't realistic? These falsehoods are not something God would lead you to be seeking after. Trust the Word of God and engage in the light of His purity. A step in His direction always proves fruitful in the spirit and the heart will recognize a good adventure from the start. Looking like a sailor in the wind with no sail does no one any benefit. Always look at the plan and expect God to work through you. If you have a willing heart, He will do exactly that. He never engages where He is not welcome so be sure to love the Lord with purity and a motive of goodness. Otherwise, all is for naught. The slideshow of hope will come forth into clarity, and you will realize where to step. A map will be clear, and the ground covered will be square in such a way that there are no loopholes of doubt or blank intuition. Lean on God's wisdom and engage in truth. You will be blessed when you do this form of action.

_____

_____

_____

_____

_____

_____

_____

_____

_____

_____

Talking is a way to communicate. All words spoken hold truth a time or two, but none of God's words are ever false. He is great and steady in all ways. You can bank on His honesty forever, amen.

Look at how the Lord carried His people through the desert. He was never late in bringing them food, water or lodging in the form of tents. He kept them clothed and secure with a path forward. Due to their own ways, they lost sight of what God had in store for their future. It would have taken mere hours to gain entry to the promised land had they only been faithful without following false gods. They stepped outside of the Lord and lost sight of who is good and faithful. They expected Him to act a certain way when that was not the plan they suffered with doubt and lost hope. Going against the Lord never proves fruitful. Even if one is walking a path of steady praise, he may end up looking outside of the given direction because he wants things his way. When you are wondering if God is with you on a project wait for His voice to direct a path of righteousness that leads to His glory, and the rest will come easy. The vision will be there, and you will understand how to go about each laid out issue with care and understanding. Never doubt the Lord has a plan and it is good. He will guide with direct contact in the form of a heart pulse and you will know His will. There will not be delays or dark thoughts of cheating or personal gain in the form of rebellion from the King. He only grants favor when things are aligned and in true connection with His heart. Look at how the people of the Bible understood who to speak with in times of wonderment. They turned to Christ and prayed with an earnest passion that was intended to reach the ears of God and present Him with meaning from the heart. You must be in prayer about all needs, and clarification will come. Stopping the prayer chain brings about a lack of witness and you lose the surefooted attachment one gains by speaking directly to God Himself. You can accomplish much through attending to the connection you have to God. It will bring pleasure and security with a directive for each day. Jumping ahead is a misgiven way to engage in any practice. Show strength and let God lead you to goodness and mercy. You will find both a delight and you will dine on understanding. This is how God operates. Know this and know peace.

_____

_____

_____

_____

_____

_____

_____

_____

All of the sudden things change for the better, and you realize the wait has been worth it. Holding on during the process is difficult at best, but with the Lord you are granted a contented heart that basks in the understanding He is with you during the process of growth in the spirit.

The Lord has never forgotten a promise or a curse. If you follow His direction your steps will be tried and true. If not, you will fall under a line of discipline and not know where you are being led in the dark. God is the bright sun and moon. He is not a defense but a true worthy passion of light where truth lives and grows in peace. If you question His guidance perhaps you have fallen victim to self, inflicted pain created when you take your eyes off the spirit that guides you with clarity. God will never ask you to wait until you no longer see a gift as something worth building for. He will move before this transpires within your heart. You will know clarity and walk in the right way because God does not want for you to fail. He is not one to tarry or cause heartbreak where love and fortitude should grow. God takes seriously any gift given to Him from the heart. You can always count on a return if you manifest your work toward His person. Showing a connection to your King will grant you wisdom and opportunity. You won't lose if you stay focused on Christ. Every day you wait is a step toward strength and circumvent delivers one to clarity. You can find all you need in a quick manner if you trust the Lord to open the pathway and lead with truth. This never fails the heart. Always trust your God for He is good and true. A step away will lead to nowhere of importance or purity. All you know to do should relate to the King and His ways. Taking time to pray and listen builds in one the pathway where light and meaning meet. God will always provide solid understanding when you know His will. He will never change course or ask you to go against anything you know to be true in His Word, the Bible. Look at what it has to offer. The spirit will know truth when it hears it unless it is clouded with self-preservation in the form of lucrative desire for personal gain. Always hoping for a fast cash flow is not of God, nor is the plan of attack designed to hurt another. These will never be gifts from God. Start today as the beginning of understanding truth. You will go far if you do this practice daily.

_____

_____

_____

_____

_____

_____

_____

The people of today are simple in their thought process. They think on what they desire of themselves not what God wants for them. God is the one who knows the plan for all steps, and triumphant manners that will lead to a goal of beauty with a plan of hope as a result of calculated patterns and plans of wisdom.

Your thoughts and hopes are not contingent upon your own commitment or the commitment of others to you. They rest in the hands of God, and He patterns them in such a way that all lead to a second season of growth when multiplied in the form of good will. You can characterize a good plan when the steps that you understand are right and true. There are no variables that look bleak or questionable. There is only light with a guidance that shows the heart where it is to step in grace. Nothing looks like a step backward or in the wrong direction even if money is questionable, you will have a process where income can flow forward, and claim the land of opportunity in the form of pockets that are well fed. You won't wonder where your monthly income will be acquired from. There will be a path that shows you clarity, and a strong guidance will be understood. Your questions will all be met, and there won't be any blank holes not filled in with understanding reigning true. Think about what pleases God, and you will have insight as to what may be His direct course for you to take. Each hour of understudy in the Word helps to form a picture of how to go about phases that will produce a clear picture with fruit at its core. If you have no clarity, try reading a few verses from any book of the Bible. God will guide you where to find a message of hope so you can step in faith and begin the process of growth. There may not be a handbook on what you are attempting to do but trust will bring God into the scene, and He will take over the issues at hand. Nothing is questionable when purity is the marker for your steps. Taking a stand for Christ is always a positive format to follow. You can't go wrong when you are placing your faith in the hands of God. He will carry your thought process to the light, and He will dim the parts that need to be removed from your mind. Each step forward will make it clear, and you will see where God wants to place your ideas and goals. Trust Him and He will guide you into a submissive understanding that leads to success and a provision not yet known.

_____

_____

_____

_____

_____

_____

_____

_____

Today we will see the stars and the moon but not the whole planet as a complete circle. With God we are able to understand steps of a plan but not the entire process. When in doubt stand still and wait for God to reveal a step in its entire format.

If no understanding of how to make a plan comes together is within your mind, perhaps you aren't the one who is supposed to do the building. A natural process is when all the pieces fit nicely, and a square of truth is in place within your spirit. Looking for ways to bring about an endeavor will lead to a mishap and a gift of doubt and despair will ensue. Let God be the one to form all the procedural implications, and the needed format of how to go about a new development will gift the mind and you can step in faith. If time passes and nothing new is developing, then it may be time to rethink the order you have begun. Is there a unity between what you are thinking as well as a gift to the individual that bears witness to a plan of good return in the form of mercy and grace outside of the monetary goal? Are you expecting the Lord to lead you with clarity but have not taken a path that leads to the throne? Should you act in such a way that there is a new directive or are you stationary because God is at work? It takes time to build a great ministry when there are no previous goals of achievement to back up the undertaking. If God is at work, you will have peace about Him being the one to develop the stages because they are out of your league. If you are thinking you are supposed to gain a piece of property, but you don't have the means to provide the expenditures then wait and trust God to lead. He may have a different viewpoint than what you see and know. This will be difficult as you won't have control of the outcome, nor will you be able to build all you desire the way you understand things. Letting others know the plan can bring about an inspiration you haven't been privy to. God uses many to enforce a new outlook or growth experience. Should you wait too long you will lose the objective, and your focus will expand in a new direction. Take what you know to do and step in faith.

It may be a simple aligned heart who needs to hear what your mind is centered on. No one person stands alone. God will control the outcome so don't be afraid to venture into the unknown. Your footing is not dependent upon your own manifestation of the spirit. You are guided daily, and all you encounter God has a plan for. Seek Him in prayer and let Him influence your decision making. There is great strength when a goal of unity with another is applied, and action is taken.

_____

_____

_____

_____

_____

_____

_____

_____

Today, many think wisdom is found in a book other than the Bible. This is false and straight from the liar himself. Except for a few ministerial readings nothing but the Word of God can reach a soul and gift it with knowledge. All material must be from God alone if it is to produce a sound measure of unity with Him.

Seeking to know God better results in hope and clarity that bounces the will of God straight to a person's heart and mind. You will gain an opportunity when the door of justice opens wide, and a vision of purity begins to form. All your efforts will count as acts of grace, and they will be seen by God as solid and true if your focus has been Him and not on material gain. A little effort put forth brings about much gain, and an added insight that only a child of God can realize. If steps have been before you, and you have covered much ground, you are on the right path. Even if it takes years building for the future in a labor that speaks to the King is never without a battle of wills at some point. You may desire for a rapid beginning along with a quick middle so the end result can be seen swiftly but that is not the way God builds character in a person. One needs the battlefield to learn how to stay steady and moving at a pace that offers a growth pattern of divine understanding. If a door opens too quickly one jumps and dives into the deep end without a solid understanding of the treacherous body that awaits him. If you step with intention but allow time to build upon each problem or gain, you will realize there is only one true form of gaining rewards that last a lifetime. A personal commitment to Christ is much the same in the way it brings love, and a forthright attitude that induces a mature mindset for the betterment of man toward himself and his King. Seeking a plan of goodness always results in a positive outcome. It may be different than you had envisioned but, nevertheless, it will prove to be righteous and meaningful. Looking at the beginning stages of a plan only relay the first impression not the picture as a whole and how it can benefit the party involved. Today you may like the color blue but next week you may have a new desire, and the color blue has lost its flare in your heart. This is minor but it reveals a talent for change that can enhance a body and gift a spirit. God has made man to desire change. He grafts man to be like His nature with ideas and paths of hope. However, God is unchanging in the way He governs His people, and the way He operates and thinks. He is the same God of yesterday, today and tomorrow. You can count on Him to always be fair and just with love at His core. Take time today and relearn the importance of having faith. It will guide your steps, and hold you close to the King while you wait on His guidance from this point on.

_____

_____

_____

_____

_____

_____

Look to the heavens and see the Lord in the stars and the moon. This display speaks of unity, and a path forward is understood in the grace it offers. This happens because God has a plan even for the atmosphere. All the stars align and are placed near planets that rotate with ease. God can do this because He is supernatural.

Crowding a bus is not wise as there could be a wreck and people will lose their lives. The shelter it offers is a simple shell not a sturdy embankment that houses with care and safety. God is different from this structure in that He can protect against all limits. Never doubt God is at work building for you a safe haven. He caters to any who submit their cause for the sake of Jesus no matter how involved it may be. Looking at order brings clarity with a plan forward. Match what you know to be true and build upon it in faith. A simple note to yourself is a reminder of what is needed for groceries. This is a practice done by the wise. The mind struggles to contain all the necessary remembrances as it cannot do what it desires at all times. God on the other hand remembers all things with ease. He is a crafter who builds the steps forward for any dream. You can hear His plan when you breath in His knowledge by reading His Word and applying the principles found therein. Accept what you do not know, and let God bring about a plan that entails all the subject matter in which to craft greatness. Even simple steps such as prayer bring about clarity. Take time and embrace the Father through the witness you offer when you trust His direction. You can do this by simply meeting Him at the altar of truth and directing your step in His direction. You will know you are on the right track when clarity is revealed, and you see with clear vision how to proceed. If you are waiting for a miracle, God knows this. He can provide all you need in a simple act if need be. Otherwise step in faith and take action in the form of unity with His character. Your crafting and building will shine, and you will be granted a life of liberty where freedom is at your door every day.

_____

_____

_____

_____

_____

_____

_____

_____

_____

_____

The soul is pure when God is the one it is focused on. Looking to complete a task will fall into place when you engage in the Word and look at scripture on a daily basis. This produces the necessary understanding of who the Lord is and how He operates.

God's work through a person will never blossom unless the person is ready to receive what the Lord has in store. If you are attacking another or looking to reward your own pocketbook you will never know the love of God and His person. He shies away from darkness, and those would not be light within a person's spirit. God knows who is willing to serve Him, and how they plan to operate each detail that He invests in them. Never realize another outside of the true King as Master. Only one individual can be the true Messiah. Jesus Christ is that person in the flesh but also God personified. Take what you know to do and apply your heart toward the truth of what the Bible has to say concerning all things. You will never be in doubt about a course of action when you entertain with the Word of God. It teaches and instructs in the form of spiritual recognition that graces one in understanding. Knowing the Lord is a gift offered to all of mankind. Only the wise understand this and accept God's guidance. No one ever has a master plan unless God has revealed it in full disclosure. God offers insight when the time at hand is the directive, and the lead is seen by an individual who is trusting in what God is offering to his spirit. Recognizing this is a process learned by applying all you know to the good of the spirit. God will act when He is ready, and all things are in place. You can't rush the process. This is what leads to a lost opportunity and in its place is confusion and a misstep resulting in loss of time or more in the form of depression and fatigue. Carry your heart toward the true King, and feel the directive gain understanding when God calls you to action. You will find it a place of wonderment and hope. There won't be heartache, nor will there be a loss of motion going forward. Each step you take will lead you right to heaven's gate. This is a matter of speaking but the representation is understood. Your clarity will be rich and true. You will hold a wisdom that you hadn't known before. Craft with care and trust the Lord in all you do. It will refresh your walk and graft you closer to the true King.

_____

_____

_____

_____

_____

_____

_____

_____

Today is an adventure when the heart trusts in the King and lets Him lead with faith at the forefront. Each moment that you expel doubt you gain an approach of unity where you are joined in the power of the Lord and His person.

Listening to God speak can only be obtained when one trusts in His power and domain of interest. If you study the Word, you will realize your God is faithful and true. However, He never works when someone professes to believe but truly just is in it for the ride. God knows who follows Him in faith, and who trusts His direction. He can calculate a solid understanding in a second's time thus bringing about change that is for the better. Craft in unity with the one who doesn't leave your side. You will gain an option of declaring Christ as Lord each time you invest in His work for the Glory of His person. God never builds where He is not welcome. Waiting for the perfect opportunity takes patience, and a hope that only God can provide. Look at how the Israelites suffered as a result of miscalculating who to follow when they took their eyes off of God, the one who served them well all through the dessert and the traveling they ensued. There was never anyone who starved or lost footing on the ground they covered. All were safe and restored in a fashion only God could have deemed fit to offer. The people were shaken by a simple loss of meat, and they acted as though none would ever come. God provided quail in an overabundance, and man gorged himself and became sick. This is the nature of a sinful heart. It desires its goals to be achieved before a balance is underway. Man fails in the area of procurement. God alone can bring about a plan and execute a delivery where all parties are blessed and secure in the outcome. Attempting to build in a fast manner leads to dark developments where failures develop and bring about a loss of trust between the people involved. Everyone needs guidance and the Lord offers it freely. Take a look at your surroundings. Do you see a stable setting or is there room for improvement? Are you worshiping in faith and following the law of grace, and trusting God to provide your needs? Do you believe He will act according to His Word? Should you act in haste to meet a goal? This will bring heartache and sadness to any executed act that isn't offered from God, and His mission won't come forth by your hand. He will choose another, and you will lose the designated opportunity God put before you. Call on Christ and let Him know how your heart is feeling. He will speak and reveal what the next step is you are to take. He is faithful and true to His Word. He is a leader and a guidance counselor.

_____

_____

_____

_____

_____

_____

_____

The ghost of the spirit is not a fable. It is true and it reveals the Word of God when you read the Bible. Without the spirit known as the Holy Ghost you won't understand what is written. The contents won't be clear, and you will have confusion. A simple profession of faith in God's direction will bring clarity. Pray and learn the message of the cross. You will be saved when you do.

An example of this is from the book of Amos. He was granted the light from the Lord when He embraced the spirit of God with his whole heart. Jesus is always with us, even in the Old Testament. You can read this truth in Genesis for in the beginning He was with God at His right side. The two have always been one united and strong in all they do and see. You can't hide from Christ, and who would want to? He is glorious and just. Never does He come against any who love Him. He is faithful, and His purity is a shadow of greatness not seen by the mind until one accepts His gift of salvation. For those who doubt this is true, it is simply because they refuse to let God reveal Himself to their spirit through the Holy Ghost. God is never one to interfere unless He is asked to join in participation. God draws near to those who place their trust in His leadership. He is talented beyond measure, and He grafts His heart to anyone who calls His name and requests His presence within them. If you doubt all I have written, what is holding you back from testing the truth of this? Are you afraid it will happen, and you will then be under Lordship? Does this frighten you? If it does, you do not understand who Jesus is. He is a kind and loving being. Never does He impose a harsh measure against those who serve Him well. You are always serving someone whether you realize this is true or not. You are either in the camp of the Lord Himself or you sit unknowingly within the site of the enemy of God. There are only two teams. Many don't desire this to be true, but it is reality even if you don't believe. Is it worth the risk of finding upon death you chose poorly and now do not have comfort or hope forevermore? Stay connected and lean on the King. He will guide you and you will know His stance for every decision you need to make. He crafts with care, and He never fails. Walk with Him and learn all there is to know in His Word. This takes practice and a committed undertaking. God will hear your heart as you read, and He will listen to your cares. You will be blessed with knowledge, and clarity to your life will unveil in such a way that you never doubt who is Master and who is servant. Fortunately, the God I know is gentle and loving, and He cares for His people deeply. You are rich when you know God.

_____

_____

_____

_____

_____

_____

The stars are sparkling even in the daytime. God has them on stand-by for the evening residue of glare, and upturned beauty that will encase a heart when it sees the dancing.

Look at Paul, he was a man God used after his blindness was removed. He never understood who Jesus the Savior was before the plan of God revealed clarity to his mind. In much the same way you can gain insight only once God has declared your witness to go forward. Each thing you encounter may build upon itself and grant you a realization where hope lies and how to achieve a goal. God can bring about a plan within minutes or He can develop it through a process of growth with blocks being placed one upon another. If you are at a standstill wait and see what door opens for you to walk through. Trust the direction God offers through the wait time. There may be growth needed for you to have character that stands strong against adversity, or a ground of hardy dwelling may be revealed. Your stamina may be needed to carry the load that comes before your path. God never holds back without just cause. He doesn't elevate one only to tear down his witness before a stand of deliverance takes place. He will craft your heart and teach it duration as that is His goal. He desires for man to never fail or lose hope. His methods are right and true. He knows the many steps that are needed. Perhaps behind the scenes is a clear development that has to happen, and you have no knowledge of what this may be. Trust God to brighten your path while you wait. Find joy in the simple tasks of your day. Look at the provision that is on your table daily in the form of groceries to the belly. Remember each provision is grace on a platter. Should you desire to understand why the standstill ask God to help you have clarity about a long, term, management skill. You may learn you are to be used in a unique manner where the gift of leadership is what is forming. If you lead, there are many aspects required before a solid foundation is cemented into your spirit. This can happen by way of experience or God can bring this understanding through developed skills in the spirit. Your character is important and until it is steadfast with Christ, God can't bring about a leadership stature due to His reputation being on the line as well. Ministry holds a gift for the soul. God will use a person when they rise up and act as the Father Himself would under adversity. This training ensures a stand of faith that produces a mature outlook that grafts one to another without any falsehood. This is what God looks for when building a structure of integrity. Your heart needs this in place or it will fail a mission and lose the focus of Christ. Remember God knows what is taking place within, and He organizes a fruitful outcome when character is right and true.

_____

_____

_____

_____

_____

_____

The more you embrace truth the better your life will be. God is always the one to guide in this area of growth. Trust in His way and be refreshed. You will find freedom when you realize He is a giver of finances as well as benefits to the spirit.

Remember the Lord grants hope along with financial freedom when you pursue His direct implements of unity into the hour of purpose. This means you need to underline and score the reason you are chasing a dream. Is it for personal gain or are you hoping to reach many with the plan of action you are trying to bring about? Taking what you know to do and building it with care is a necessary contribution that allows one to engage in a witness of understanding and experience. What amounts to a tally of untold riches is how you perceive the true King. Is He a giver of all you own, or did you amass the wealth without His being the benefactor? Realize God is the one who lines the pockets and brings wealth to a man's table. He will do this if there is a commitment of the spirit where your pride is not a factor, and you haven't brought about a falsehood or a delay in the form of deception. Your grave matters where it is dug just as your history counts as a heritage. It can either be a unified step with Christ or it can contain a fragment of dark clay not conducive to a burial plot. This analogy is quite bleak in the fact the body decays and is destroyed over time. However, your spirit lives for all eternity, and that is where you work to be with God. If you haven't applied your mind to the recognition that God is the provider, and He never leaves one without supplements of some kind, you don't know the God of the universe. You only know about Him. He is a caregiver who loves His children, and He delights in giving them riches. Gold is not His focus, but He does reward hard work and an aptitude for good measure. You can find the gift of generosity written about in Samuel. He found treasure in being a servant of the Lord who delivered truth to the people, but this doesn't mean God didn't provide. Look how He planted him in a place of security when drought came upon the land. God is ever faithful, and brings wealth when one applies the truth he has learned to his life in all good standing and unity with the Word of God. A little bit of pleasure can lead one on a path of darkness. Remember to stay connected with the King and the desire for sin will disappear in short form. Walking the way of the Lord is a gift offered with every page of the Bible. It will strengthen you, and you will discover a great release and outlet for true ownership in Christ.

_____

_____

_____

_____

_____

_____

_____

_____

People mourn and feel helpless when a person leaves the earth and is no longer alive for fellowship. Taking a look at what God is all about will grant a closer study in the Word of the Bible. This is the place of unity with the true King, and this is where love is always found.

Let's walk in faith and express the truth of what God teaches on a daily basis. Take the steps to engage with the spirit of the Lord permanently and forevermore. Grafting your will to His brings a balance and a drive that contains all of the qualities God holds dear. A drought may come where you feel disconnected. This is a result of not looking at the Word and reading its contents regularly. Before every endeavor look at wise counsel. This will ensure an opportunistic desire that coincides with the will of God. He has formulated the spirit to join with Him in a presence of mind that wills His love directly in line with His way of thinking. Never lose your way again. You have the power to always know where to look for hope. Fortitude will accompany your walk when you trust the pathway that leads to an open door which will reflect the King Himself. You won't see a gate that is closed as your only option because Christ cares about all you do. He never sees your flaws as risk factors when loving you. He grants you peace, and harmony because He is a man of His word. Man in the flesh but God in spirit. He never forgets just how to accompany your every step. Taking true direction from the one who knows all is a brilliant maneuver. You can trust the God of all things to look at you as His own. He cares for you as a flower that is delicate but with strength enough to conquer the world because He is your King. This is what triumph looks like.

_____

_____

_____

_____

_____

_____

_____

_____

_____

_____

_____

Today brings a hope only God can provide. A willing heart knows His love is real. A person can gain insight in the simple practice of recognition that there is a God who has plans for his witness. This brings joy to the believer. All he hopes for is because of God if purity is the goal.

Think about the good God has done that is described in the book of James. There you can find truth about who to worship, and how to proceed with the knowledge that God can deliver on a promise. He crafts with care and exceeds all entanglements where love is truly placed. Nothing is worse than forgetting to honor the King you know as Jesus. That is when you forget just how great He really is. He will always be faithful, and He will never forget a bounty He has offered to the mind or the heart. God never leaves a dream on the counter of forgetfulness where it rusts and decays away in time forgotten. That is not His way or His mindset. He carries the load of truth with each step you take to honor His glory and His greatness. Looking at an opportunity as a gift is a step in the forward motion of faith. God gifts one with hope, and dreams that build when they trust the King to deliver and perform as the dream was delivered. You can't gain a pattern of faith when you always look at a situation with doubt. There will be times of questioning, but if you continue to pursue in faith what the heart desires God will deliver a true understanding when the time is right. This, however, can be a battle of wills. Waiting and trusting will produce a character of true perseverance that leads to a spirit of determination crafted into a longterm commitment never to be broken or charred because of strikes from the enemy. He will lash out at you with darts of fire hoping to break your will and bring you to a fall. Stay focused in the truth of the cross and gain a perspective where hope is always prevalent. This only happens if Jesus remains the focal point of your thoughts. Entertaining doubt casts a shadow of reluctant authorship as to the true ruler in your life. Let Jesus lead your steps and understand He will always lead with a direct course of action, even if you can't see it at the time a path will be there. Once God determines the time is right your vision will clear, and you will understand how to step. Trust God is at work, and He never leaves your side. This will ensure a positive, growth pattern that will lead to a location of love and a witness of God's greatness.

Think on the ways God has graced your spirit. Are you without a Master or someone to lead your heart as you wait for instruction on how to build a great work of art? Have you ever been without when it comes to spiritual guidance? God offers this freely. Pray and be in grace. The power is God's alone.

A look at all the holdings you have acquired brings into focus that God is at work in your life. He is always masterful and true. He never leaves you without an idea to solve a master plan, but it may take time to develop. Housing goods and services is an example that God is on the move. He has seen you prosper enough to create a collection, so this indicates He knows you are ready for the next transaction to take form. If you are at a stalemate read how David handled a battle plan. He always prayed and trusted God for the details. He never thought he was the one with the power. He believed it was God who sheltered him securely, and who gave him the insight and strategic know-how to gain a people and their land. God is a provider. He will deliver a multitude of goodness when things align in just the right order. He can multiply your holdings with just one phone call. You can gain a property with a simple friend's donation or even a death can bring an inheritance. You never know what will stir the Lord's heart and cause Him to forward an opportunity to your situation. He crafts with care, and He builds with a purpose. He won't tarry unless growth is needed in some form or another. Think how He worked in the life of Samuel. God spoke to Samuel with a clear voice. He will do the same for you. Pay attention to all your mind encounters. Are you thinking on a perspective that celebrates in the worship of your God? Are you planning for a just cause? Do you need a direct blessing in the form of truth to take shape around your thought pattern? All of this can hinder what God has in store. Although there can also be hinderance simply because there is a witness being produced. Your character may be being built upon in the form of goodness and mercy. You may gain ground by applying the truth of the Bible to your daily steps and management. You may find a breakthrough in this process. The gateway to God's heart is knowing who He is and what He desires for your life. All people are treasured by the King. He wants to lift up all of man and bring him into prosperity. That doesn't mean great wealth. It means treasure of the heart, and an aptitude to honor God in all you do. Reflect today on who you serve. This will give clarity to your cause and a bank of interest will be gained.

_____

_____

_____

_____

_____

_____

_____

The soul is not perfect but with Jesus it finds a place of importance. God is the one who bears witness to your recognition. He is the Master who plays the fiddle, and your song is heard. Your true repentant heart will reflect love if the repentance is real.

Attacking a character is not God's way of rehearsing the past. Learn the steps of gratitude and look to the Father for consolement. He will grant a reprieve of clarity as to how to proceed in the way of growth toward a perspective of unity with him. He does not want to bring harm to anyone. That is His nature and structure. His heart is different than man's. Man will try to divide a person from another. He will try to separate and form sides of interest to his person alone. If you are sharing your sorrows, remember God is the caretaker of the soul. He is the one to burden with your heartache. He doesn't mind communication and a repeat of the story being told. He hears many outcries all day every day. He can handle it. Give Him clarity as to why you feel outraged. He will make right whatever wrong has been done to your person. You need to understand when doing business, you may encounter a battle against your person. Trust God to deliver the answer and how to graft a caring outcome. He can change a person's mind or make a correction that you haven't thought of. He never forgets a wrong, but He doesn't harbor a grudge. He clarifies how to move forward and who to hold accountable. A shield of protection will surround your knowledge, and you will know how to handle yourself and present a true representation of God Himself. If someone has been misjudged, truth will come to light, and the situation will be rectified. Trust God to offer His true counsel. He is there for your witness even when you have been wronged. God will bring about a plan that pleases your gifted hand of knowledge because He holds truth as a top priority. Never accuse a person of wrongdoing until proof has been provided. Your witness may be tarnished in the event you are wrong. Give God the glory and seek His guidance as to how to claim what is supposed to have been your gift. Let Him be the one to take action and to move hearts. He can do this with a simple move of His hand or a whisper from His mouth. Stand strong against adversity. You are a warrior for truth as a person of Christ should be. Never forget who formed you. The great creator shows love in the form of unity with His spirit. When you hurt understand He will make right what is wrong in one way or another. Give God your cares, He will honor you with action. It may take awhile, but the wait will prove true for your betterment. Standing in the wake can be difficult but God holds you steady against the wave. Look at how Jesus was crucified. He was innocent but victorious in the end. Remember His sacrifice, it was for all mankind even a sinner like you and me.

_____

_____

_____

_____

_____

Each individual passage of the Word of God is true. In much the same way is His voice to your heart. If you listen, He will guide your thoughts and bless you with clarity. He will instruct, and He will give hope. He never badgers or bullies one. He is ever faithful and true. Look to Christ and gain hope everlasting that will shower you in times of need.

Today people think all is well. They aren't watching the many signs before them. All around the world God is declaring His witness is strong. He is aligning nations according to the Word of God in passages that hold true in every form. There is nothing that the Lord can't do. If you are hoping for a new adventure where you are complete and whole, something that speaks to your spirit in grace, trust the Almighty to grant you this favor. All you need do is look to Him for guidance and the delivery of what is needed will shine forth. He will direct your moves and guide your thoughts all day every day if you let Him do so. This happens when a person makes the decision to trust the Savior, Jesus Christ. It isn't a loss of individuality but a joining of the heart in a manner that is conducive to truth. You won't lose hope or be gifted a lie. All understanding will be true and beneficial to your cause. You must, however, be on top of your game when it comes to worship, and trust in the work God is doing. Don't look back or question how, just set your mind in truth that God can do all. He is great at miracles, and He loves to be recognized for His good care and instruction. Give God the glory and let Him be the one to open the needed passageway. He will do it in His time frame, and you will know He is the one who made it happen. Be at peace with the decision, it all rests in God's capable hands. Don't try to lead or overtake what He is purposefully handling. You can't outdo the Savior. His love is so deep you will always be under His wing. The steps needed to learn may not be what you expect but trust God has your best interest at heart. He would never bring hardship to your cause if it is just and good. The Lord is perfect, and He does magnificent things. He is greater than you can even imagine. Trust His guidance and be rewarded with His instruction. When the time comes you will know God has delivered a sound investment with a budget to match. He cares in ways you will never recognize. Some you will know but some will be hidden. He is a crafter of many divinities such as love and care of the spirit. The match of truth will light, and you will be carried to a balcony where the height is beautiful, and the witness you give will be solid. God's purpose will shine forth, and you will proceed with care. You will be sure-footed knowing the Savior is your friend.

_____

_____

_____

_____

_____

_____

The power of the Lord is translucent with a mark of clarity found only in the Word of the Bible. Each time you turn the pages and take in the understanding of what is written you gain truth that produces a heart of integrity. You never have to worry about who to serve because the letters in red point to His person. Christ Jesus is King, and He will serve you well.

Rehearsing for a play brings one to the point of understanding the words they must know by heart. This practice assures an actor he will know his lines and be prepared for the show. All those who assume the ability of caretaker or grounds keeper understand their role is that of a caregiver. Focusing your energy on other people brings to the heart a life of good measure. When you build a business, you need to realize all you do is for the benefit of those around you. Yes, you also receive gifts as a result of working hard but this is because God has designed man to feed himself by his labor. If you recognize God is the one to reward a job well done, then you understand the benefactor is not you yourself but the King Jesus. He will accompany your thoughts and set in motion a clear and precise way of acting and carrying out tasks for each day. Follow His guidance and you will grow in truth right along with prosperity. God promises both in Jeremiah. Taking into account the Maker in all you do will support a measure that only true worshippers of Christ understand. If you are confused concerning how this may be, read in the Psalms and gain a spirit of clarity. God releases good character on the pages of His Word. How this happens is by His design. I can't explain it but I know it is real and prudent in all I do. I never doubt God's Word is written for the benefit of growth, and He never leaves one confused or without a purpose. Things may take awhile to fall into place, but the order is a necessary measure that only God completely has control of. He is gracious and will deliver on the grounds of His good name. He promises to never leave our side. If we walk in faith, He carries our thoughts and dreams and makes them a reality. He is the Waymaker, and you can be assured of the importance your desires are to Him. He will craft with care and never leave you stranded. That is not His way nor is it His way to step aside when you have reached a plateau. He is at work. Be still and wait for the truth to reveal itself. God is crafty, and He can make all good things come to light. If your wait is unsure, prepare in the way of prayer. Ask God to speak directly to your spirit and conscience. He won't fail to embrace a pure movement His way. Leading a blind man is not His way. He gives the blind sight out of love and respect for the people He holds dear. That is who He is.

Teaching others to know who God is gives one the heart of a warrior in as such a spirit of truth comes forth that declares God is real. Never doubt your King is with all you do. He never leaves your attendance, nor does He leave your spirit. He protects it and balances all your mind has to offer in the form of thoughts or guidance.

The tally is long when the Master has control of the time clock. Yet, through the process of waiting, a clarity is formed that reaches into the depth of the mind and offers it understanding. If you are waiting for a miracle, remember God produces results that bring into focus a truth where none existed before. Only He can bring change that reaches the heights of heaven. In this process you gain enlightenment that catapults the mind into a divine, manifested organ that can regurgitate the Word of God. Only scripture can enlighten the true message of hope that God offers each individual on a daily basis. When you embrace this truth, you witness growth where none was before. This growing process is a real statement to whom you serve. Every detail you learn is a manifested work of art the creator engaged within. He spoke clarity, and truth in the form of a spiritual connection designed by His hand to reach you personally on a level you can relate to. God speaks in different forms. Many people hear a voice directly to their heart. Others engage in reading, and He fulfills their mind with truth in that manner. Still there are people like me who write, and the words of truth just flow onto the page. I alone cannot write a truth if my life depended upon it. Only God working through me can graft this great stance. I don't seek to know or understand all the ways God can communicate with us, His children, but I know He does. There is no denying His abilities are but a fraction of what we ourselves can do. I never want to forget He watches over me and takes steps with my person. He shows me the way and enlightens my thought process so I can understand where to turn. He doesn't take away from my own personal being but He enhances it. I cherish when we write together but I know He serves me in many other ways as well. I pray to engage with His spirit at all times. When this happens, a bonding takes place, and a real enhancement of unity is presented to both He and me. If you are looking for growth, engage with God in the form you can relate to. He will meet you there, and you will feel His presence. He will move so you understand He is with you.

_____

_____

_____

_____

_____

_____

_____

The looking glass is clear, but the sand is white. All of the grains are pure in their shape and formal structure. God has designed them to be rough but small under the foot. Combined together they don't bring about pain, however, one by itself can pierce the eye and cause it to water. Do you understand the principle this portrays?

Each person by himself is not significant in the work he does. But when you combine the talents of many great things can be accomplished. Doors will open, and a uniform understanding will take shape. God allows many to have a place of their own but often times He builds such a grand operation that many are needed to bring about a plan that offers good measure. Buildings require contractors of all sorts. They are the building blocks to the foundation. If a place of business is small, it may need just one person to operate its communication throughout the day. Each is purposeful and productive when God is the focus of the fruit they produce. Leading a team of people is not for all. God raises up those who will bear the burden well and do His bidding. If you feel left out or looked over, perhaps a new train of thought is what needs to take place. You may not have the skill set or the mentality to host many people under your wing. God chooses who will climb the ladder of success by way of gifts and talents He offers to the mind. If you want a better position, think on how you can come forward and build a better position in which you now hold. Show leadership skills by working diligently for the owner and watch what God does for your outlook. He can graft a heart in such a way that boredom isn't there even if you do repetitive work over and over. God is a caretaker. He is someone who lays before man the opportunity to expand. Even if you are limited in your current abilities, ask God to change your situation. He can do this quickly should He desire to. Don't judge another for the work they do. Remember Jesus was a lowly carpenter and look what He accomplished in just one day!

_____

_____

_____

_____

_____

_____

_____

_____

_____

The flowers of the night are not a dark presence but one of beauty. Some unfold in a pattern where multiple hearts hear their decoration. A spoken word of truth is not a word of doubt but one of fortitude where the Lord builds a heart, and makes it stand with clarity.

Today people run to-and-fro. They believe they're the ones to bring about clarity within a community. The blindness they have is a pattern granted by the one who decides what is to be known or hidden from the heart. God does not bring about a path where little is known or reflected upon with care. He crafts the passage where a mind gains a limitless guided understanding that brings with it a true measure of growth. The enemy often tries to enter the scene and place obstacles in the path of growth. He does not want for a person to do the bidding of Christ. He wants him to fail, and to think He can't press on even under pressure or time constraints. God will never limit the growth of a heart or make conditions where there is a start, stop process. God delivers clarity in the form of a guided hand that escapes the lie put forth by the enemy. He shows man where to find the truth. Think about how God operates. Does He ever limit knowledge from being revealed? Does He mark a certain percentage to be designated just for Him or does He make Himself available at all times? Does growing in the spirit require a limit for the day allotment? Never does He do such things. You can learn and be fed at all times even if you are weary or under pressure. Perhaps that is one of the best times to hear the Word of the Lord. Building this book has brought to light that there are many ways to encounter truth. Looking at the Word of the Lord is the one true way to have sure-footing. God will speak when a problem presents itself. He will make it clear when the enemy is deceiving you. His voice will reach your ears so you can have clarity. Remember God is always at work building in the form of greatness. When He acts, people are granted an insight to His character. Even when the light seems dim, look at the power of just one verse from the Bible. It can free your thought process and entertain truth immediately to your spirit. God never fails. He is true and a glorifier of what is good. He can build with ease and grant favor with a blink. Trust His good ways and know He will always play the part of a provider. He wants you to prosper and to grow. Sometimes that comes in fast and furious but not always. Sometimes there is a pace that is set that brings balance, and a growth of sturdy measure. Both work according to Christ's design. Both bring clarity and both are free. Guidance is a gift of the spirit. God won't hold back this fruit when you pray and believe He will grant it. He loves to honor prayers. So, look forward to just rewards because you are faithful to communicate and cast your cares in God's direction. He will respond accordingly.

_____

_____

_____

_____

_____

Growing with confidence is a gift given by the King. He plants hope and prosperity in the mind and configures truth to reach the inner most thought processes of man.

Look at what the Lord has done in the form of beauty all across the globe. He has written His true character in the view of man's heart, and He instructs the mind with clear teaching. There is none greater or more in tune than the one who always grants His love and His goodwill to His people. Looking at Christ as the true Savior is a gift of the spirit granted with free will. No one is forced to follow the Lord. He is invited in with a calm undertaking that brings about love in the form of unity and a crafted final grace in the dimension of the heart. God always provides a clear view to His person written on the pages of His Word. The Bible contains many gifts to learn who the one who claims to be King really is. If you read and gain insight, you will see for yourself that God is good. He never sets anyone free. He holds them close and releases their spirit to a witness of grace and they learn He is all He claims to be. Never believe anyone who preaches another gospel. It will be false information, and you will be led astray and left in the dark, confused and alone. With God the way He teaches is soft and gentle. It is with guidance and a close- knit look into His spirit. He never brings on the scene a dark presence or words of stringent direction. He will speak freely with grace and a smooth tone of love with clarity that is bright and forth coming. He never puts in place obstacles to growth in knowing His person. He would never allow one to be stagnant if their desire is to build a thing of beauty that branches the love of God into a clear manifestation of hope. God always gives one the understanding that He is always available to learn from. He will feed your spirit solid direction each and every time you come to Him for learning. He is not going to open a door then hold it ajar again. That is not His way. All the Lord offers is of a grand scale in the form of complete comprehension where there is no doubt or misguided thought. If you wonder if God is upset with your actions, remember forgiveness waits at the throne each second of the day. Repentance is always the key to moving forward and being received in truth by the King Jesus. God has provided the open door to a life of beauty and fortitude. Jesus is the only way to gain entry to God the Father. He is the great Waymaker, the one who loves all and believes all to be valuable. You are such a creation. God desires time with you, and He wants to be your guidance counselor. Your steps in His direction are seen and accepted as hope for His solitude to be within you. God will act on your behalf if your heart is sincere and looking to bond with His person. Prayer gets you to the place of worship where you and the Lord meet as one. Never forget the power prayer holds in your life. You can move mountains when God is on your team. Play ball with Him and have all winning plays.

_____

_____

_____

_____

_____

The talent of man is showered in the form of a gift from the hand of God. Many play sports with flare, and others write poetry or secure a fortune with the purpose of educating others. All these things can be a part of a good measure of purpose. God can use them to bring about a plan of purpose. Let Him lead you with direct steps that He has made clear to your heart.

Your heart cries out for a plan forward, and direct action to take that brings forth your desire to come into view. God may not desire such a plan. He may have taken the path to new ground where your efforts can be better served. If you are finding no open doorway without understanding why, realize God is still in control. He still has a plan that is prosperous, and it will grace your thinking when the time is right. God may have given you a desire but not the means to accomplish your goal. Know He can bring about a new measure of ability in less than a handshake's timing. God is not one to graft to your heart something He will not bring forth in some manner or another. God is shielding you when you are at a standstill. It is His way of controlling the heartbreak of misdirection or a misguided step. He is careful to lead with purpose, and guidance that speaks of hope and a future of true worship to His being. If something is too great for you at the moment of its birth, perhaps a growth is needed in your spirit then a transformation of unity can take place. God is always at work, even if it seems like He isn't. Know He steps in faith, so continue to pray and give Him glory in this measure of trust. If you are frustrated, He will know this. Don't expect His presence to be removed just because this time of trial has you feeling out of sorts. He will guide your thought process and bring you clarity for the moment at hand. He may even open the door so you can understand just what is needed for a better viewpoint. You may have an interest in something that is harmful or not of the caliber you should aspire to. Grafting in the form of rebellion is never a good, direct move. It only brings a loss to the situation. Jumping ahead of the plan brings pain in some form or another. Let God lead and bring you clarification with a measure of hope alongside the standing He offers.

_____

_____

_____

_____

_____

_____

_____

_____

_____

Teaching the Word of the Lord is a gift to the spirit. It can come like the wind in a rush, or it can be a whisper to the heart. But either way, one gains a clarity where there once was confusion or no real gift of unity with God. Always look at what is transpiring in the form of growth. If there is union as presented by order, and clarity with the gift of love, you know you have proceeded correctly.

Wherever you look God is busy grafting people to His person. He is bringing them into the light and producing a good measure. If growth is what you desire let Him speak to you in a personal manner. Something will click, and you will soon realize the plan is before you. Trusting the process God has underway is what comes as a challenge, yet it delivers so much clarity. Never doubt, when silence is underway, that the voice of God will continue to speak. He adjusts in His own way for man to gain an insight about how to proceed. He never leaves one alone to discover how to step on the outside of His person. Even if you are blind and have no clarity, trust God will deliver on His end an open gate for you to walk through. If there has been a time gap, perhaps a new plan is being formed because the old way was a misguided dream you thought you were privy to. If God wants you to know how He is working, He will make it clear, and you will understand the truth of the situation you are in. Relax and let God do the work. He is a master creator with all the guidance one could hope for. Never doubt He will perform on your behalf a measure of unity that correlates with His desire. Always keep in mind your work is important to His personality type. He never forgets what direction to take, and He knows the best way to go about it. Latch on to this true way of thinking and you will understand your Savior wants the best for you. Even though you aren't able to identify the workings at all times in the end you will acknowledge the workings He did were true and fast. Enjoy the process and hold fast to the knowledge that God will conquer your fear as He is a warrior of hope. He never cheats a person, nor does He set one up to fall. He grafts the spirit to His so goodness comes forth in rare beauty. If you feel weak, engage in the Word of the Bible. You will gain strength, and you will be set free of doubt. Trust Him, He is faithful to the core.

_____

_____

_____

_____

_____

_____

_____

_____

_____

Tonight, the moon will set, and you will see the pattern of a face embedded on the surface. It will look bleak but visible with a clear appeal to the heart of man. God has designed this look of the moon to bring about stories of true inspiration. He enjoys a tale of character with truth at its core. Anyone can design a grand display of opportunity if freedom of God's grace is the purpose.

Talking in parables was God's way in instruction to those who knew His name and the condition of His heart. Anyone who approached Him with a clear set of instinctive responses that were true and just, gained His following. If you have not been faithful to the pursuit of the Savior, you may not be understanding a directive He has given you. If you are working and things are building upon themselves, then Jesus is your focus. If a project is on standby, perhaps there is a cog missing. No one knows better than Christ how to manage a situation. When you ask God to give you a vision of truth, remember it may not be what you thought would come through. It could be a matter of a new developed outlook that boasts of integrity, and a useful understanding granting favor when the time is just right. God will speak and He will direct each step that is needed. Sometimes it is a matter of longevity. If you feel crushed in the wait, decide to release the dream, and trust God to answer when He deems fit. He won't waste a moment on a harsh takeover of the mind. He will wait for you to desire a new list of requirements or translations. No one is in themselves a deliverer of goods or services. God always is the one to raise up an opportunity. He puts it on the platter of love, and keeps it safe for distribution when the setting meets His standard of time. Waiting can be troublesome when you have struggled to grasp the cause. Never doubt you are of use. Perhaps your wait has more to do with the fact another is slowly progressing, and they are an instrument God will work into your program. During the process, God will implement other directives. He will give clarity as to these purposeful attributes you hold, and He will assist in the knowledge that you serve Him in multiple avenues and strengths. Listen for a guidance you can relate to. This will be the true calling for you to express the work you desire to do. Even in a time of rest God brings about a plan. It is up to His direction to know each detail and how to implement all things good and just. You may be hidden from the scene for a while, but an awakening is sure to come. Give God the glory while the process is underway, even if it means nothing is happening in the area of interest that you have control over. You may have invested much for a dream. Let God make the motion come. He will move, and a rich development will take place. Under His wing is a safe place to be.

_____

_____

_____

_____

_____

_____

The peace that comes from truth is a gift understood by the delivery of God's spirit to your soul. Every thought process is a claim to the spirit of whether one trusts the Father or whether he trusts himself. If one accepts the lead of God Almighty, he will never be without a companion who is faithful.

You can know God through the process of prayer and engaging in His Word. If a sounding board is all you need, then read and listen for a direct communication from Christ to your spirit. You will realize the mighty hand of God touching your life in many aspects when you wait for the spirit to move and give you clarity to your issues or concerns. He will never direct you to do something against what His Word declares. You won't hear a voice say, "Come follow me" into a temptation of illegal standing or misguided good deeds. A fast buck does not guarantee a solid bank account. God can build with little to no grafting in material wealth. He can open a door and lead the hand to wisdom where a field of delight holds grain in the form of growth that inspires and directs all in a form of simple faith. Trust the one who supplies the needs of man no matter what the standing is in the community. You can't hear God call if you are focused on material wealth alone. Yes, you can pray for money to flow toward your desired skill set, and that you would be blessed by it, but know money is not the objective the Lord holds as most important. He is looking for a material witness of a different kind. His desire is for you to understand His person, and to meet Him at the cross on a daily basis. He wants to feed you with hope and purpose that leads others to the throne of God as well. He never leads in a direction of outer bearings with no guidance or clarity. There is always a plan in place that is secure with its layout. Granting time toward the Father is a wise move for anyone wanting clarity in their daily lives. You gain wisdom when you pursue His great being. None can compare, and none can contribute to the cause you are hoping to secure better than Christ alone. He knows all and sees all. He sends His angels to surround the people who step in faith, and who hope to correct their walk and make it true and forthright. Never be a person willing to gain ill repute earnings. This will not bless the spirit, nor will it invest toward the kingdom any real earnings. Let God show you when and how to distribute the income you gain, and you will be blessed knowing He has provided fruit for the family of God through your endeavors. Hoarding all you own is not beneficial and it causes you to lose focus on the true inheritance from above. God is the reason to work or to apply your progress. He is the great creator and benefactor. Remember He never fails, and He guides with purpose. Be on His team and grow with aptitude. He is a Waymaker, and He has a plan for your success just as He does for all mankind.

_____

_____

_____

_____

_____

All the stars align, and they are beautiful in the manner they hold. Their presentation is a delight for man as he gazes at them during the evening hours. You can gain a truth in the scripture about how God built the universe. You will find He is a master crafter and a true source of inspiration.

Talk to the Savior and learn His voice. Understand He crafts with care. He loves your companionship, and He desires to know your heart. He waits at the corner of truth and care where harmony of the spirit can be found. He never goes against His person, nor does he incorporate a lie just to better Himself. Learn from His example and gain a perspective that offers a true formula for gaining a look at how He maneuvers all things for good. He is true and faithful. He cares for all man, and He is always working on their behalf. He is gracious with a dash of personality that speaks of good cheer and a gain of influence for the better. You won't go it alone if you undertake a build that leads to a birth of genius influence. God is the one who grants this favor. He never admits sin to be good, so don't try to take short cuts. He won't deliver in your favor if you do this type of practice. All man sins but it is how you decide to proceed once that sin has taken place. Is it habitual or a one - time offense? Are you trying to make it right, or taking steps to ensure your name is removed from the practice? God knows and hears how you desire to operate. If you cheat and lie to get to the top, expect a balance of ill returns. You can find capitalism is a hindsight if you struggle with good measure. Balance your heart, realize God knows all and He does not desire deception. If you trust Him for clarity and a purpose, you will find a gift of lucrative hosting at your door of understanding. Take what you have learned in the business world and invest in the grace God puts before your mind. You will build with clarity, and a host of opportunities will present themselves. Your platter will grow, and a perspective of faith will ensue. God is a caretaker, and He grants others this skill set. If you find many people rely on what you have to offer, note you have been put in a place of honor. Don't abuse what you have been given by the King. Engage and offer faith alongside prudent gifts of delight that bless others in their direct correlation to the King Himself. If you hide your faith, others will not see who you serve, nor will they believe you honor God. Having faith can be difficult at times. Trust God to protect your standing and give Him permission to direct your steps. You will gain bounty when you do.

_____

_____

_____

_____

_____

_____

_____

People of today think their importance is greater than the real-life God we all serve. They think their understanding of unity is to be at their peak when it comes to performing a task or maneuver. However, the fact of the matter is, God is the one who designs our steps and gives us the talents to perform them.

Every shelter ever built was by the hand of God upon a builder. He is the one to incorporate a plan and make it come to life. He develops the thought process that brings it to life. He is the standard of the craft. No one ever thinks about a great design unless God has grafted it to their mind. Thank God for what He has placed in your path that is good and holy. He never puts disheveled work into the forefront or balcony of the thought process. He is grand and He decorates with a grace that offers a person a way to build with character. If you're shooting to gain a fast path in the direction of God, be an understudy of His caretaking. You can do this simply by applying yourself to reading and gaining knowledge in the Word of God. It seems simple to do, but many forget this step and they find they are lost or without direction. God gives clarity with purpose. His steps with you will bring balance, and a smooth transition from one form of clarity to the next. If you find you have not progressed, think about what you are able to do right where you are. Today may present another set of instructions that build upon what is to come. Look at the process underway. Is there anything you can do to improve the floor plan you have been given the understanding to? Is there a doorway that leads to more growth yet is not the major one you are hoping for? If so, you know where to look for clarity. The opening will be available, so step through that passageway and wait for more truth to be revealed. God builds with care. He will keep you moving in the forward position in one form or another. There is much He offers to anyone choosing His leadership. He won't push or shove His will. He will simply guide and lead with a gentle touch. A little work today may mean big rewards later in life. He grants me visions for pottery I do. I build and create not knowing exactly what comes next, but I continue to create knowing God can use what comes from my hands. He is ever faithful to appreciate our efforts. His ways are true and just, so it makes it easy when it comes to having blind faith. We just need to let Him be the one to bring about all the pieces to the puzzle. I haven't perfected this stage in the wait process for all my endeavors, but I am continuing to pursue God for answers. He will speak when He is ready, and then I will rest in the work He has created within my heart. Seeing without believing is no sight at all. Recognize God is the one who delivers unity and bounty at the same time. If you're lost or confused, step into grace and hold the reality that God is on the throne. He will hear your thought process and deliver a pattern of true gifts of knowledge. This will calm your spirit, and you will know He touched you directly with a calm appeal that granted wisdom and unity with Him personally.

_____

_____

_____

_____

Teaching comes in many forms. Some are schoolroom experts while others, such as myself, glean notions and truth from the Word of God, and what He has through the spirit.

Working for God takes many forms. It can be done over the phone or even behind a computer desk. Some write while others do physical labor. Some plant and some harvest but all are connected in the way they bring honor to God, and what His purposes are, for each one carries merit. There is no need to think you aren't important. A harvest can be brought about by a simple measure of unity to Christ in which one understands his true calling is a gift from above. You can't find a parallel in the way of good measure unless you recognize God grants all different kinds of talents to His people. This is what makes a united and bonded body of believers. Thinking you are special is true in the way that a child of God is purposeful and direct in their way of life. But thinking you are above others is false and misleading. You can't operate in true clarity unless you see that God is the one who leads and boasts of good returns, for He is the one who manufactured all there is to know or comprehend. A shadow of a man can bring to light where the lamp is positioned, but he can't make it move unless God designs the act to happen. I know this is a simple example, but it speaks to the great detail in which the Lord works and operates. Even the smallest of gestures is designed by His hand to be an offering of unity to the body. If you have trouble including others in your circle, try viewing them as respected individuals whom God has ordained to know His person. An envelope is not the letter it contains, but nonetheless its purpose is vital to the witness that is presented. Each note of music brings to the ear a sound that glorifies and edifies the true nature of a song. Without separate parts to a whole collage, nothing of beauty can be seen. A leaf has veins along with green vines. Both suggest it is fed by a source not seen to the naked eye. We as people can glean a true perspective that incorporates hope to others if we first surrender our individual hope of stardom. No one is great except for Christ alone. If you have fame remember who has placed, you in this status. You may fall just as easily as you were raised up. Take the liberty to evaluate the offense of a dealership who has robbed people of a true price range. Will they be rewarded in good measure? Will they find peace on judgement day, or will their dealings show their need for riches out surpassed their faithfulness to God? No one escapes their actions of the past but those who truly repent and set an example of purity, will meet Jesus and know Him as Savior of his soul. I for one will hold fast to the administration of the Lord Almighty. He is the one that grants favor. He is the one who serves me well.

_____

_____

_____

_____

_____

The tally of the mind is not calculated by your own thoughts but rather it is seen and heard by the Master Himself. He is the one who shows all just what is needed to accomplish a goal on any given project or work of bounty.

Today many guess the time for expanding is the way to gain a prosperous living. But if you knew just what the truth of all dreams came from, your outlook would gain a new perspective. God the Father grants dreams and visions. He calculates the order for each to give birth, and He delivers its course and action in sure form. If you work outside of instruction and think you are the one doing the work without guidance, you represent a fool's mentality. God not only crafts all builds, He designs every element therein. Taking it upon your own understanding will lead to a depraved mindset. You can't go forward when looking back. This applies to the standard in which you incorporate the King in your everyday way of being. If God holds no place with your endeavors, you won't have a stance of pure just cause working in your corner. God grafts His intellect within the spirit which in turn determines the mindset and order of things to come. Granting favor is a job offered to few. With it comes the need for a clear vision as to how to gift others in such a way that joy comes in the process. Gifts can range from wealth to garnishment of wages depending upon the need for any situation in the sight of man. God views work as a promising way to make a living. He honors this stance, and He secures employment for those who are willing to earn this gift. Never doubt someone has been promoted because God knew an inside track that you couldn't perceive. If you find favor in His sight, rejoice and celebrate. God benefited you in such a way that you could blossom and grow. A harvest isn't always grain or fruit. Many times, it is a crop of thoughts and actions that lead to a wise handout from God above. Knowing when to reap and when to sow can be described as a gainful opportunity that unfolds with a purpose for growth or individual gain of the heart for you or others around you. Take a look at the detail surrounding a baker's rack. Each loaf of bread had to be blended with flour and milk so the yeast could grow and produce a rise in elevation. In much the same way God, plants yeast within your spirt. He supplies the necessary staple for a balance of good return along side an appetite for true clarity into His person. Your yeast is His wise counsel. It rises when the heat of the oven is turned up thus resulting in good character and a mature outlook on life and all it holds for you personally. Give God the credit in your daily walk. You will be blessed with the process, and true growth will shine in accordance to His will and supplication.

_____

_____

_____

_____

_____

_____

Let there be guidance in the way of the spirit says God who created all things. His Word is a gift to man so he can graft Biblical understandings and glean an opportunity to undertake a way of life that is purposeful with hope at the helm.

Talking to God through prayer is a way to communicate with His spirit and tell Him about your day. Each word you give Him to host celebrates a kinship that is honorable and trustworthy. You can find a balance between your words and His when you look at the power His Word holds. You will understand there is much to be gained when you apply the teachings of the Bible to all you know and do. You will learn a principled platform of unity, and a way to administer to others in a simple and clear witness. Growing in the truth can happen quickly when you believe what you read is true. If you doubt the scriptures, you will lose control and a dark admission of deceit can gain a foothold even when you think you are paying attention a misguided front will appear. Every teaching tool ever needed is in the scriptures. They contain much in regards to living a life of purity. Balance doesn't happen if you are seeking something other than what should be assessed as pure and just. Deceit has a limitless amount of promises but they are all false and lead to death. You can't serve two masters. One will prevail and you will succumb to its directive whether it be hope and clarity or a bounty of forgotten measures with no merit. A category of sight is a blank mat for the mind to sit upon and gain insight. All God offers is parallel to none. He is the only side of influence that offers real peace and joy. If you find these gifts appealing begin a practice of study that relates to your schedule. If free time offers breaks and times to reflect, look to God's Word and use your set of parameters as a guide to manage your free minutes. If taking a nap is a joy but you rest then desire more from God, He will honor this practice as much as one of complete pressing measures. So, don't think you can't learn because you have no time for yourself. God knows the heart, and one that serves Him with a pure motive is what He favors. Be it a small endeavor into His Word or a porous amount of study, you will grow according to your effort applied. Each person grows in faith only by the guidance of the Holy Spirit. Invite Him to apply His workmanship within your soul and you will gain an exact replica of the one called King. It comes into completion upon death for the believer. All others are cast aside, and they never achieve true companionship with their God. If you aren't following Jesus Christ, you are following outside of Him and that means Satan is your father. The father of lies will never complete a pattern of truth, nor will he let you live in faith. So, look to God for faith, and a balance of trust will incorporate a hold on your life, and you will be granted a place at the table of the bride. This is true in all you do, so apply your strengths toward what is good and solid in its claim for the King. You won't be disappointed or forsaken. God is just. He will follow His Word to the letter, and there are many to learn from.

_____

_____

_____

_____

The battle of wills is difficult unless one listens to the commands written across his heart. God will speak a true and clear message and you will personally understand what that message says. Always assume your Savior is a caring representative who has your best interests at heart.

Closing patterns of doubt come into play when you haven't taken the time to read the Word God has in store for you each day. He never brings one to the edge unless they haven't taken to heart His teachings in a manner that is conducive to love and honor. Accepting a word as truth must be tested and tried against what the Bible has to say about the topic in mind. If you are finding a closed path and there is no light, perhaps your mindset is waiting for a dream that is not of God. You can find clarity in the many conversations written with true appeal that contain an exact measure of needed insight with just one passage. The Bible contains the means of lucrative gain, and a balance of integrity that compares to none. Should you desire gain to be ill gotten, a life of acceptance may reside on your shoulders but where will it end up leading your heart. You can't steal from places and expect to shop there when the truth becomes known about your disgrace. Remember the King is never satisfied by slavery of sin. It never engages His spirit, nor does it bring a clear unity with His person. God will respond in kind measure when you give Him faith with sincerity and a clear consciousness. Never doubt He will see all you do so running from His person is pointless. Step with unity and grow in favor with each mile. A treetop does not see the light until it reaches outside the reach of other branches when it is growing forward in faith. In much the same way you can't acquire a golden endeavor with the tool of deception. God honors steps of gradual increase where He can bring growth in the way of spiritual awakenings which grace the knowledge center and inspire the home of the heart. Never doubt you are bounty to His spirit in the sense that His love will forever be true to you. You are a child in whom He cares, and no one or thing can ever disrupt this fact. Today, many feel there is little they can do to contribute in the making of rich wealth. However, wealth is a tool strictly seen as a means to gain more material affinities. God operates differently in the way He devises a plan and brings it into the light. He leads with a vision that engrosses the heart to be better and to delight others as well. He never wants a person to be so focused on the aspect of gold that they lose sight of the true opportunity before them which is to know the God of all things and His people too.

_____

_____

_____

_____

_____

_____

Making a plan is not always the only way to develop a technique where there is proof of your authorship to the devised outcome of growth. When God works through the process, you gain a realization He has authored the plan and the phases are by His design. He crafts with ability, and He never makes a mistake.

A market is small when there are few buyers for the goods you offer. However, God can bring about a plant that blooms in the form of a market where many purchase what you have to offer. He does this with those that perform in faith and trust His guidance. Looking to Him for clarity is the best solution to learn where deception may be present. There may be an influence that is at work that is not honorable, and God will reveal the culprit and remove it at will. Paying attention to the Word of God enables one to move with grace, and it brings to light any darkened area that is hidden in the mainframe of your mind or actions. If another is the culprit, God will remove them when He sees fit. It may happen with a distinct manner or perhaps a behind the scenes move will transpire. God is honorable in all He does so expect Him to keep what He holds dear in clear view. Working with God grants the eye an understanding that the king is clever and shrewd against the enemy, Satan. He is the influencer who brings about destruction and a negative vibe in business dealings. You will never honor God if you accept bribes or a material witness of doubt, for bondage of the mind comes in these forms. Clarifying how to operate before you hire a manager is sound judgement, and a precise understanding can come forth in this practice of management. Letting another govern over your wares may require a close scrutiny that they may not be aware of. People hide in the shadows when they do wrong, so don't expect your employees to come forward and confess theft. They will think they have mastered the art of stealing with each coin they rob. This is how sin operates. It breeds lies one upon the other until total captivity of a drunken brawl is executed. This may be in the form of jail time or perhaps the loss of income for many decades. If you are known as someone unreliable the word will travel, and your reputation will breed, and you will be thrown out of the public eye. God won't lift you up until true repentance takes shape, and a clear desire for a pure reconnaissance is forefront and center within the makeup of your heart. God grants favor to those who are true and fast in their love and desire to balance their moral lives with their work lives. Both must speak truth and be holders of good character.

_____

_____

_____

_____

_____

_____

_____

The palm of the hand is intricate, and it holds many things at different times all depending on what the desire at the time is. God hosts dreams and He builds them to become a form of beauty in which no one can deny He had a hand in the matter. Trust Him to build you a dream where your heart rests and grows in a manner that only you understand.

Let today be where you accept the limits of your abilities. Make it a day of wonderment where you talk with the Savior and ask Him His plan in all you have underway. If He provides you with insight, then you know you have reached a moment of grace at which you will find a home in the production department. There will be a notable piece of understanding that wasn't there before, and you will dine on clarity. Even though you may not have all the pieces in a pile, what you do contain in understanding will lead you to the next step or perhaps even show you how great your adventure will be. God never leaves a person to hang on the cliff without a rope to propel down the side. It may be a challenge with a difficult maneuver for you to handle, but God does not lead in a manner not conducive to His character. A plane has wings but needs a pilot to fly safely to its destination. God operates with this principle. He does not offer a valuable ministry without first equipping the leader with skills to have a successful harvest in the form of fruit for His people. God grants all the opportunity to be a leader in the witness program of love and good measure. You can find truth when you read the book of God's Word, and in it is all you need to know to share the Gospel. Christ Jesus is a Master at all He does. You won't find Him lacking any skill set or in need of advice from anyone but the Father in whom He is joined. They are a team, and they offer many ways to know their person. Looking for ways to build may come in the form of an undesired thought that breeds to a mindset of clear representation where you find you actually love what is happening by way of the Father's hand. He crafts with care, and He offers all the way to learn more of His person with simple prayer. You can do this anytime anywhere. Your mind operates as a tool of instruction, and it can be a worship center as well. Think on the goodness of God and honor Him with praise. He hears every thought process, so don't think you can hide a negative viewpoint concerning His work in your life. If you pay attention, you will realize He offers your heart's desire you just haven't been able to recognize this is true. Many have learned God the Father is loving and kind, and He never produces a plan that isn't a blessing. Craft your mind around His good nature and watch what develops. It will be pure and good with a spruce tree of flavor that entices the spirit into unity with the creator our King Jesus.

_____

_____

_____

_____

_____

The look of a person is based on the desire to appear pulled together and at ease in life. Your gifts or talents come from the King. He is the one who blends a unique character with a dash of perspective to each soul. No one is ever a solid representation of the Father but for Jesus Himself. All others who aspire to know God look for truth and clarity at their core.

Growing a temple takes many people to do the work and spread the labor between the gifted hands of each participant. If you alone are hoping to accomplish a great build, look at how God operates when forming a city. He creates a suburb, each distinct and natural in design. He does not build chaos but a definite pattern of uniformity. Well-crafted buildings bring a look of success and hope to their formation. God wants for you to have the same presentation of the heart. He desires you to invest in His spiritual goodness far and above the look of the exterior or hardware of the body. He never forgets a gesture that was directed to His person or a seasoned prayer that had the words of beauty straight from the center of one's mind. If you are genuine and true you will not be sitting in wonder where the Lord is leading your steps. You will realize He is at work building for you in such a manner that your focus will be united with His drive and forthright character. Look at where you have come from. Are you a believer with strength or do you lack the gift of endurance? Are you wondering will God ever move or are you waiting and expecting a plan to unfold? Has a building block become an obstacle because it is daunting and a ritual you need to progress through? There are many reasons for a waiting period that may or may not be something tied to you personally. A struggle to know just what all is taking place brings the heart to a low comprehension of the character of God. He does not wait on a person without a specific mentality that guides with a lucrative endorsement toward hope. He may have you engaged in a work outside of what you expected to be doing. He works in mysterious ways sometimes. Crafting a big design is laborsome, but God is not frail. He can craft in a moment's time, or He can build in sections at a time where you see results unique and different in manner. Know He cares and He delights in working with you. You can't go wrong if you engage and trust His direction. His shadow is straight, and it never misses its target. It casts a line of clarity and direction without there being a need for doubt or distrust. Never think God won't move. The timing is what matters, and He knows all the ball players on the team.

_____

_____

_____

_____

_____

_____

Teaching skills come from the aide of the Master's hand. He instructs in many forms. Gifts of the spirit guide the mind and fill it with understanding. Taking a class can bring about a practice that offers a known segment of truth. However, only God can direct a person to lead with clarity.

The party of truth is found at the helm of the head of Christ. He never makes a mistake. He does as the Father guides Him, and this leads to a pure innovation where hope lies with gratitude and clarity. Do you ever miss the assumption you were not gifted to believe the power of God is real? No. You dine on this truth. God gives clarity, and He teaches all of man how to grow and learn in one form or another. Classes offer education that is contained in written materials and diagrams. God teaches truth in His word, and He guides the spirit with knowledge according to His timetable. If you find a distinct way of thinking brings to you hope, then you have found the place God wants you to participate in, meaning you are connected to His way of thinking. If, however, your plan is of a destructive nature, your joy is false and misleading. God never wants to harm another or to bring sin into the picture. He formulates good materials that harvest bountiful undertakings that are true and just. You can find many opportunities to do bad but if you try to grow in this manner all will fail. God is purity, and this is the way He wants all of us to operate in our daily lives. I can't stress enough our God is grace and love. He is not dark and evil. So, go on the path of good wisdom and true marksmanship. You will find it fruitful for others as well as yourself. This is how God operates. His way is of doing good for all His family. Even those who don't claim Him receive only goodness from His hand. Why is this? God never produces evil. He is holy to the core. A God of great beauty and justice is what He is composed of. Graft yourself in the knowledge God will honor you when you honor Him. It is His nature to do so. Counting the ways He has brought you joy can call His spirit to yours in a unity that brings the message of pure excitement. When you feel His presence, you realize His care for you is of a grand scale. If you weigh the good against the bad you will see how He has cared for you all your days. Even through tough times He plants His heart near yours so you can engage with His person. He never fails to bless, even under attack He stands strong. Trust His direction and let Him lead you with clarity. You will be surprised at how trustworthy He can be.

_____

_____

_____

_____

_____

_____

_____

_____

The power one feels from God above is gentle, but strong. It teaches, and it says truth always. When in doubt look to scripture to better comprehend how to proceed.

Taking to heart the Word of God gives us the needed comprehensive meaning to what we are to do. It never leads us to a dark perspective. God will always shine light toward the direction He wants us to follow Him in. Looking at the Word will rejuvenate the inner part of the soul. You will rejoice in the true meaning before your mind, and clarity shall be understood. Crafting in grace is how the King operates. He is not a dark cloud with no water. He is full of ideas and leads as to what may bring about a uniform comprehensive bounty where gifts are abundant. Never get upset when God moves the direction you are headed. It is for good measure and sure grounding. Things may look different with a new design as to what is to come about. God grows our thought process. He grants a design that is good and pure. He never builds in a dark cave of doubt. You will desire a good measure, and it will present as such. The door may not open right away, but it will be there when the time is right. God moves according to His timetable not ours. A lengthy gap may not be a harvest period, it may be a time of concern or drought like written about in the Biblical days of Samuel. God always provides, and He never leaves one without a true calling. He may be building steps and a new design element may need to be completed before the whole picture can come into play. Recognize the feature of truth. Are you accomplishing good measure and sturdy groundwork in your daily life? This is important to recognize. Never pursue a thought that leads to a ground network of dirty laundry better known as sin. This will compound the time it takes, and you will be frustrated and discouraged in the wait. God offers one the ability to gather his thoughts at any point and time. If you have fallen, take a step back and look at how to proceed in the light. You can stop sin immediately by refusing to pursue it any longer. Slip ups are a way of life for any person. How you handle this fact is what declares who you are as a person. No one is innocent. No one leads a perfect life, and no one can claim victory without the Lord's help or His strength upon his person. Each step you proceed in the right direction will build upon itself. That is where true support of grace comes in to play. Without it we would all collapse and claim death because the burden is too great to bear without Jesus our King, and His death upon the cross.

_____

_____

_____

_____

_____

_____

_____

_____

The battle of a completed design is not just of the spirit but of the physical body as well. Working in the fashion of true networking can bring a build to completion in a quicker manner. Realize people need people to grow and build any development big or small.

Working alone is not God's way for His people to live. He has not designed the heart to bear witness just to itself. He does not desire for man to be alone in His life, invested opportunities, or his many adventures. His desire is to craft a heart where man engages with many throughout his everyday walk. If you are a loner, perhaps the spirit is leading into a division where you grow in the form of communication thus resulting in a new developmental stage in your craft. If you wait on people in a store this is networking. If you desire a personal design element, such as counseling this too brings a person close to another. They both serve a purpose and have value. No isolation factor need be a control mechanism. You can simply visit your neighbor or post online. In this way you are reaching out to others and offering a part of your spirit. Communication comes in many forms. God grafts the knowledge of what is needed for a relationship to grow. He will speak to you with ideas of how to bless without it costing a fortune. It can be a simple "hello" to an ailing friend or maybe a card with an enclosed written inscription from your own handwriting. This always shows you care. Little things are what represent a faith, even in the slightest form they teach those around us that we are a people who trusts in the Lord, and His personal guidance in our walk is proven true. When God directs the steps, a pattern of love is showered. Even when we least expect it, a plan of beauty can unfold as a result, and we will see a seed planted or a soul harvested for the kingdom. The power lies in the arms of Christ. He is the one to deliver a message or a prayer. We need only trust His directives and learn His wise counsel, so we know where to turn and how to step. He offers this with freedom, and His course of action is always true. Read the Word of God and engage in faith. It can carry you to heights not before seen by your witness and study. Grafting to God declares you are His faithful follower. He desires nothing more than to know you better and to hear you call His name. Dine on strength by committing your heart to Jesus. You will encounter a purposeful mindset and a desire to be more alert and attentive to all who come your way.

Resources come by the hand of the Lord. He is the one to fill a bank account or to breach a contract that is unholy. He will always bring to light a debt or a misguided way of processing the facts of an undertaking. He is faithful to precure any needs to make an example of greatness in the form of unity to His spirit.

A message from God to your spirit will host an undertaking of clear view with a distinct motivation to share who He is in some form or another. This can be accomplished with a simple plan to reach another person through a material witness of good measure, such as bringing to them a spiritual notebook or a word of prayer that they aren't even witness too. God can move in many forms. Don't limit your viewpoint by thinking small. Dream big and be a mighty warrior in the battleground of a thought process. Prayer is the way we engage with the Master. It is how we develop a relationship with Him personally, and we gain insight through the process we undergo during our time with Him. There are many ways you can pray. Be it a simple act of a bowed head and a few words lifted up or perhaps a message of the heart where you speak to God through your actions and intake of thoughts. He hears both. Always realize you have power in any situation when you serve God faithfully and in a true manner. He will always come to your aide if you are righteously pursuing a good cause or deployment of hope for another. Even if you think your actions are limited or funding is scarce don't be stunted for lack of innovation. God knows how to make things happen. You don't have to worry about how or what. Just offer your spirit to His mission and let Him do the work. Is this not an example of what faith is all about? His Word clarifies we have power in prayer. He speaks of how it can manifest within His grace and supply the needed component to build a networked parliament where He can act. Why He chose this mechanism is not for me to know or comprehend. It simply works just like His Word says it does. Advice from the Word of God will always prove true. Banking on this information can carry you into an understanding that you alone can bring about a change because you will enlist the power from above. If you are in line with how God operates then the earth will move and shake for you. If you are not don't expect any kind of reward or growth. It is a simple math equation God first, loyalty second and respect third. With these three components you offer God purity and that is who He is always and forever.

_____

_____

_____

_____

_____

_____

_____

Each tally is a gift when measured by the cross of truth. It will decorate the understanding, and lead with a true purpose in which the heart grants the mind a unity and a hope. With God one can find this in all he does if his heart is steadfast in Christ.

If you study the Word of God, it grants you with a capable way of measuring goods and services, so you never have an empty bounty with no cash allowance in the tank of a unity where God serves you best. This process is not new in that God has always made clear how to serve Him with the proper mentality and goal insights. God is the winner in all He does. Every move He performs is for the better of His people and Himself. In this He teaches a true grit type of mentality that adorns the mind with a clear unity of pure wisdom only found by the hand of the one who makes the world go around. God cannot ordain a minister if that person truly doesn't care about the witness contained in the Word of the Lord. Each word printed and crafted is true. It is an amazing piece of intellect, and a memorization in which all of man can obtain truth. Many don't realize the gain they can have multiplied upon their social score when they trust the King to be their worship center. Your heart calls to the Lord above, whether you acknowledge this is real or not it is a fact. God designed all of man to worship His person. It is what separates them from all other forms of life. Animals are made for man. They have been designed for us to eat, wear their skins and serve their needs in the form of growth or cultivation. Man is not to abuse their existence or treat them poorly. A sacrifice is made when an animal is put to death in order to bestow sustenance in the form of nutrition of palatable gifts to the mouth. Never take for granted the love God has for His creation. He won't allow death to be a pleasure in the heart of anyone who trusts His leadership. If you find yourself working with the offerings of animal life, count it as good and true discipleship from God's hand to yours. Each person who engages in cruelty on a basis of hate is not doing the will of the Father. They are simply harvesting death upon their own personal self. God sees and knows the spirit. If you have taken a life out of protection of property or even in self-defense know this is not a hate act. Population control is needed so that life may sustain itself. The cruelty expressed by a poacher is not an act of life- saving measures nor is it needed to control an overgrown bounty of living organisms. God knows the difference, and He will desire for you to as well. Keep your Bible as your guide master. It will teach you every answer you could ever want to know as far as a lineage and grouping of right and wrong. Your daily walk will be enhanced when you do this practice.

The new way of thinking is for people to think they are the ones in control, but in reality, they are just a fly in comparison to the power God holds in His little finger and that is stretching it. The grace of God is far bigger still.

The memorandum one posts to his subconscious is a gentle reminder to never step outside of the one who created you. It is there, bold as ever, when you are about to sin or step within a range of destruction. It matters not the degree or caliber of the intent. There will be a tug at the soul, and you will feel a slight unrest in your spirit. You will know something is wrong with the plan in motion. This should cause you to stop and process the element that is causing the discernment. Don't ignore this instigative measure God has bestowed upon your spirit. Recognize it and back away from the desire. It will fade, and you will no longer be tempted beyond your control. Think on the things that bring life and a positive climax of unity with God's spirit. He never holds you captive. He allows you to walk in the way that He leads but know the more in depth you desire to know Him the more you need to stay clear of what you lose control over. If a drink has become too much a part of your daily intake stop the process of buying it. When the supply is not readily had it makes it easier to keep a balance therefore keeping you in control instead of it controlling you. This can apply to just about all we do. Remember God has a plan even for the lost to know Him. Our example of how we deliver our hearts to the presentation of life reflects on our ability to reach the spirit of someone who has addictions themselves. You are a light. A beacon of hope. If you are pressed to continue to take in a substance that isn't edifying, you aren't spreading hope but despair. Others breath the same air. When one is weak, they set an example of weakness. When one is strong, their light shines and gives off a hope for the other party to recognize as power from above. You can lose your way in a simple step of commitment in the wrong direction. Balance your intake and make it plain you are a warrior of the faith, not of the enemy. His way is dark, and it leads to death. Should you need relief look at how God built His family into a strong pillar after they fell from grace. His leadership showed them the power of His will, and that He cared for them even though they lost their footing. The Old Testament speaks to the great capacity of God to forgive and offer salvation. Sin doesn't have to carry with it a name and a place. Make it invisible and a faint memory. Release the power by asking for help and God will gladly give you the necessary enactments to gain freedom. He favors all who call upon Him for guidance and love. He is real. Believe His grace is for you, and you will know Him in a deeper and more meaningful way than ever before.

_____

_____

_____

_____

_____

_____

The moment you realize the work of God is what is true and just is when the light of opportunity can begin to grow. A balloon does not glide because of the wind. It floats because God rests it in His grasp and tells it where to bring about happiness to a child.

Teaching is a profession where many gain insight and instruction. Not only do they engage and participate, a true uniformity takes shape in the process that is being offered. When one learns they glean a message that contains a spirit in which the mind accepts what it is being taught. Today many are taught lies, and no truth is being given. The manuscript of truth is no longer in the classroom outside of a Christian college or home setting. Christian preaching is being silenced, and the crowd who once gathered now no longer exhibits a unity to draw the spirit of the one true God to counsel them. He alone can bring into the light a grace of enlightenment. People who know the truth of a commitment gained by the parishioners, understand God relates to the prayer of many with a sound anointment that graces all at the same time. He may speak and bring about a manifestation in which the background isn't even visible because His spirit is so strong. He may invest in that moment right into the pockets of the people with a right and just provocation allowing a permanent supply of His trust to each soul. When this takes place, a grace of love distinguished in harmony reaches the mind and clarity comes like never before. If you pray without the understanding of why you gather and what the purpose of the meeting truly is, you will miss truth when it is presented. God never absolves a soul, He enhances it with a pure explanation and anointment. People meeting in the same undertaking bring to the surface where a placement should be found. It brings hope and a communication that releases the groundwork for the bride to do a work of a great magnitude. If you pray with people who are God focused, you find yourself with fellow believers who realize the importance of a united stance in the eye of the beholder. This is what brings to light the purpose of how to work or how to develop a long-term relationship with a clear purpose. God brings people to His home where a temple or structure of faith offers a comfortable, relatable setting that distinguishes the hope of God Himself is there. This can even be a classroom setting or a couch in a living room. It doesn't have to be a church building. The body of Christ is the real church expression, and it is where life is found. A dead body does not expect God to act whereas a living body knows God will move when He is beckoned to. Trust God to hear you when two or more are gathered as one for the cause of a good thing. It is a celebration to the spirit, and it graces one with the dignified grant of a personal engagement with Jesus. Be strong and wise, pray with friends and family. You will find it a blessing and God will speak like never before. This is a guarantee He offers in His Word.

_____

_____

_____

_____

The tower of Babel was not built for man to reach heaven. It was built to try and out do God, the true ruler and guidance counselor. Man thought He could bring himself to the heights of heaven and gain all there was to know.

Tuning your radio grants one the station that plays his desired music. However, all the stations do not play the same enlistment of opportunities to hear and take in. They only offer what their own personal playlist looks like. They predetermine the background for the day and set it in motion. If one wants to expand upon the unit and discovery, they have to engage in other broadcast outlets. The same can be said for man when he is looking for true and meaningful relationships. This can only be achieved when the father enlightens the spirit as to who to connect with in a cordial manner. Relationships are built on trust. They are a square of opportunity. You either find good genes and a height of integrity, or you learn deception is the running feature of a man's heart. Take what you know and apply it to building on behalf of your social structure. Gaining ground in this area, is often times, limited as to your available location or your network of friends who invest time with you. Not all understand goods and services can also be found in the way we engage with other spirits. Man does not live alone unless he has no interest in sharing conversation or interaction with the needy. People are often broken and in need of encouragement. You can offer to help by simply speaking with them and offering them encouragement. The book of love will help to rebuild a spirit when one applies their spirit to its contents. Looking at how Jesus walked this earth gives us a better lay of the land. It is a guide, and it directs the mind into the understudy of the gravity of an unfolding display of character. God is the crafter, and He makes no junk. So, all people are built for unity. We all desire a home with family and friends. Even when some people are less talkative than most, they still connect on a one-on-one gathering of the minds. They are fed by close interaction not a full, frontal display from a crowd or large gathering. Learn your strengths and let your spirit shine. God will open doors for you to speak and share His truths. Even in a quiet setting much can be gleaned and built upon for the glory of Christ is everywhere. The hour to witness is ever before us, and we need to recognize the light shines in many forms. Whether it be behind a screen or on a stage, every communication action produces fruit. God can carry an announcement across the airways, or He can deliver a whisper. Grace is what brings about the real mechanism which distributes true recollection of the spirit of God. Your growth is not dependent on the words you spoke. It is made manifest by the power of the Lord. Trust His appeal to man. It is real and it is genuine. A piece of it will carry you far.

_____

_____

_____

_____

_____

_____

Calling for a new president offers one the hope of change and a gift of unity with his person. However, many times the man at the podium is not true or a man of his word. With God you can find a narrative that remains steadfast and solid.

Watching for man to bring a way of change does not mean you are against God. You have hope that He has placed that person in a standing where truth prevails. A quick vote does not insure the right candidate was elected. Many variables come into play when the count is taken. A true representative will calculate each tally with an honest delivery with no additions or subtractions. If tampering takes place, the honor system will reveal itself, and the man who gained a lordship will lose it to the rightful heir. God delivers to man what he seeks. If it is deception, then he will gain that exact measure back to himself. Noting this is true will get you to a place where you will desire the exact good measure for all of your deeds. You won't be tempted to engage in falsehood as you will know that it will produce the same in your circle of growth. Counting on unity is the way God presents His dispatch of good information. Clarity is gained with the knowledge God can perform miracles, and He often does. Even though you may not heed His way of thinking, you can't deny you haven't been warned. Should calamity befall your endeavors perhaps rethinking how you gained them in the first place may bring to light the purpose of your lifestyle. A tank of gas leads to fumes yet it displaces the driver from one point of entry to another. Look at how God led the Israelites in the desert. He never opened a path they couldn't follow in a way of purity and good measure. Their steps were always close to the person of Christ, yet they dispatched an alarm, and called a false god to them for the sake of security which in reality was not the hope they received. They were only acting out of fear and a heart of rebellion. If you run to the arms of the enemy, he will reward you with more distraction and a false hope in which nothing grows. You may dance on the grave of injustice all the while eating the flesh you live by. That is the technique the dark one follows. He never gives gifts that are pure or full of honor. But you can rely on the true God of the Bible. He will teach you a measure of purity that stabilizes your steps, and grants a power where grace is your right hand. Take a look at who directs your steps. Is it God or a false faith? A light of clarity will guide your thoughts when you trust the Savior at His word.

_____

_____

_____

_____

_____

_____

_____

_____

Grace is supplied in the form of beauty, and the landscape it presents is a balance of hope and true relations that parallel to God Himself.

The time it takes to complete a task varies due to the extent of each endeavor. If you want a real forage of a unique dimension, then invite God to be a part of your work program. The way He creates, and builds is of a standard that enhances the mind and body with a true character of grace. Looking at the many people who have come before us written about in the scriptures grants an insight as to how the God of the universe likes us to interact with one another. He aligns our spirits, and we perform in ways not thought humanly possible. The grant of power He brings into play dashes us to the finish line. The way we get there is tried and true. When He administers our thought processes, we entertain in a dimension in which His real person correlates for us a path of complete description with no errors of substitutions that effect purity. An ounce of doubt can bring about a fall if it is fed on a daily basis. Seeing the light of hope placed within our grasp proves just when we administer the needed faith that leads to a complete work of art. A category of alignment can be seen in the way a build is presented. The structure is secure if God is at the helm, and He directs all the plays. A team of horses run in unison with each stride of the flank. In this manner they all reach the goal of the driver because they are tied together by a rein and sheath that girds them one to another. They won't miss the court because the driver has them in his sights and he leads right and true. If a cliff is on the horizon the team is led in a new direction. God offers a path that never leads to a harness of doubt or shame. All He crafts is of grace with a perfection only He can provide. If a plan looks doubtful, remember He is the great and mighty warrior of the heart. If you feel pressured to perform an act, it is probably not the plan of the true King. He offers peace and solitude when He presents an undertaking. The gear He adjusts is simply that of a motion forward. It is not a step back or to the side. If you find yourself moving all over the board, you are not tied to the King. He is order, not chaos. Your own thoughts can bring happy thoughts but are they God honoring? Do they represent His spirit and His way of gaining ground? Look at the dimension and the lateral length of a trip. There are many highways available to make a way for the trip to conclude. However, there is one way that is the most stable. God operates in this manner. He is tried and true with precision and a diplomatic nature.

_____

_____

_____

_____

_____

_____

_____

Standing in the rain gets one wet. The tree above shelters one from the storm though it can't shield from the wet drops. God is the sanctuary in the storm. He crafts a place of security in His heart alone.

Looking at Christ as your Savior is a way to be sure you feel His presence when you go about your day. Always focus on His personality type and plan to administer this practice as your own. Clouded vision casts a dark shadow if you're not prepared to realize the true condition you are facing. God will always be able to release a sound measure that speaks of a unified practice for the spirit to engage in. Finding peace brings one to a place of distinct reality, and in this course of action you are guaranteed a bountiful harvest. The grain one reaps is spearheaded because the Savior leads with a hand of mercy where instruction can always be heard. If gaps are forming in your mind and you think you may have slipped from the course God was providing, rest in the understanding you can repent and look at prayer as a way to gain the knowledge you need to correct the situation. A climb is high if it is the mountain top you are aspiring to. God has a platform that will take you directly to the top without hinderance. It may require a stand of strength, but you will never be alone. Each step will build upon the other, and you will learn who truly carries all the weight. A look at this truth is written in the book of Matthew. He tells the heart how to proceed when doubt enters the mind. Everywhere you look you can find people who have engaged in something that brought joy or even despair. How one gains clarity between the two comes from direct communication with the one true King. He teaches man how to live a life of unity with Him and how to know His voice. He is not a blemish against the heart, and He is ever faithful. Knowing how to follow Him comes from grace. Every attempt you make toward knowing Him personally results in a true progressive mannerism, and a joined undertaking in a vocal manner meaning you can hear one another speak. Learning how to decipher between God and the enemy can at times be disheartening. Look to the tone and the way true love is exhibited. You can find this by reading the character of Christ. He is not harsh nor is He one to directly attack your personal thought process. He is gentle and loving. He offers a plan, and He speaks truth. He is not condemning or rude. He lifts you up and encourages your steps. He will not explain a harsh reality to you if you fail and commit a sin. He will offer redemption and the blood of Christ will sooth your soul.

_____

_____

_____

_____

_____

_____

_____

The network of love is heard by man when the power of God's voice reaches to the spirit within. All the power of man comes as a gift provided by the Creator who built the heavens and the earth.

Listen and you will receive a clear and direct group of playbook materials. This happens when the door of understanding is opened wide to reveal a network of good measure. All things of God are true and just. Never are they dark or misleading. You can find hope at their core, and the insight will grant favor to perfection and true witness opportunities. Even when someone works as a chef, they can bring glory to the King. A simple act of kindness directs one to show how the Lord is a reflection of this measure. Each nice endearment translates to a person in which others want to pursue. Never think for one moment that God doesn't see or hear your actions when they present as true characters of Him. The ground is not hard because of the wind, and it is not soft because of grace. These things are separate and apart from a spiritual grafting. Only God can relate to these inanimate creations of His. Man just wonders how and why it all correlates one to another. This perception is a gift we cannot comprehend. The inner workings of each detail found in nature is a mystery only God can solve. He created so much for man to engage in, yet we never conquer all there is to know about each detail. The light bounces off a reflective base and releases a beam that the eye can catch, but no unit of study shows us how this happens. God the Master, is a designer of the heart, and He knew we would respond to its clarity. If darkness persists on a hearts desire it may be due to the fact the Lord is not in it. Accept the fact and move forward toward a better gateway where the Son of man is the focal point. The funding for a project may be lacking, so this may be an indication you have spun a web of deceit even though you thought you were doing the Lord's will. It can be apparent to others so communicate what is before you and see how others respond. If they like what they hear and can see a way for progress as a result, then give consideration as to why you have developed the things you have. Was it for glory or the hope of fame? Are you content in moving forward with the prospect no one else may relate to your dream? Could this be an indicator that something is wrong? If you are alone gathering wares, be on guard that your witness may have grown into a plan of misconception in which you aren't actually the one to bring about the shoulder harness of truth in this manner. God knows how to act and when to place an idea on the shelf. A closed door can be a barrier against a dark draft that brings a nightmare in the making.

_____

_____

_____

_____

_____

_____

The tale of two wives was written to introduce the mind to a whimsical unity that is outside of the nature God wants us to follow. Man follows his own heart and falls face first into a plan of mischief and fails to understand who his Master is.

Taking the time to give a verse time to build within the mind is a good practice to pursue. A man who reads just to get time under his belt never truly hears the voice of God. He only thinks he knows what was said. God grafts to the heart when the process of connecting to His spirit is underway. The process produces clarity and a unity in which a vocation can develop, meaning the right attitude and outlook is transparent and revealed. The unity that develops is pure from start to finish. This only happens when the Savior is the one at work. He grafts your mind and leads you to the finish line in a manner that you can relate to. He doesn't lead you into prosperity, but delivers you from evil. That is not to say that riches can't be had, it just infers that is not the goal of what God desires for you on any given day. He desires for a person to develop a rhythm and be in sink with His spirit. You can trust His direction, and you can know He never cheats or distracts to cause harm. He is a crafter where all things good and honorable are in His care. Looking outside of that is not a sound way to progress. The shoulder harness never supports the muscle of the back. It breaches the back strap and divides the weight from one arm to the other, thus, bringing about a much lighter burden for the back to carry. Carrying a weight without God's support will cause a fall. Only He can support all your needs. Only He can supply a direct cause for you to gain a prize of hope where your trust is bound with His endorsement. Clarity will come, and you will gain an outlook that reaches your spirit and is connected to His as well. Timing is gifted according to how God determines the final result should transpire. You can't rush through the process of growth. It must be taken slowly and with purpose. Take a stand and believe God is available for all your needs. You will find the way to a great delivery of grace when you look for His hand in your life. His caretaking abilities are gifts, and they can be seen with clear eyes when one gives thanks and appreciates the way God has moved for him. Crafting on your own is hard work, and it never ends well. Even though you may gain ground you will find it was difficult and not a blessing to the spirit. God grants a body the gift of relaxation during the process of growth. You can find peace even as you put in laborious hours. This is when you know you are gifted with His hand upon your life.

_____

_____

_____

_____

_____

_____

The taking advantage of another's heart is cruel and undeniably a painful endeavor. If you feel led to cheat and steal you will become a lost individual. There will be no light in you to nourish another. You will serve no purpose of a sound practice so you will lose ground in the face of many.

Simple plans are the best when designed with care and an eye for detail. You can graft a segment then read the details and glean an understudy of true importance. Each detail is clear, when the Father opens the pen and fills it with ink. Your writing and critiquing skills will expand and you will gift others with insight when you set the bar high. All the world's most productive organizers prepare for many hours how to develop a day's work, whether it be in the form of writing down a list or keeping an eye on the product that is in the warehouse. A body of faith incorporates the needed craft set and displays the passage to light the field of study so all may engage in the benefits and rewards come harvest time. If you have traveled a long while you become weary. As a result, the door to strength is slightly ajar meaning you will need a time of rest before beginning to expand upon your chore list. All of the greats understand there is a time for play and a time for due diligence. A caretaker spends many hours preparing in honor of another in the form of a bountiful display of truth. Whether it be on the hind legs, vacuuming or dusting a dirty stove top, all care is a gift. Some people bake and serve in this manner, while others offer time in the field of labor over cement. Each worker is gifted in a manner they lift up others and give them relief. Some find shelter in a home, still many just offer a warm shoulder to cry on. We all have talents to offer in times of need. So don't leave your quality endearments on the shelf. Put them to work helping many find their own growth opportunities in the same manner. A person knows what they can handle and when it is time to ask for help. Often times this is difficult for people to do. But trust builds in relationships when weakness is shown. No one is superman who does an overload without crumbling or missing a step, so don't try to conquer the world. Be a member where Christ is head, and you are the bride. In this form of unity the mind is delivered from shame while the heart is embraced with a clear endearment of thanksgiving and a heartfelt unity is delivered. God can build you a fortress in the form of great friends and family. All you need to do is trust His discipleship.

_____

_____

_____

_____

_____

_____

_____

Each measurement of trust gains a person a means to develop a closer unity with the King as He is beauty in this form. Knowing the God called Jesus is an honor and a privilege. He is the Waymaker and a fruit supplier. Never take for granted He is with you or that He hears your heart.

A moment in the arms of the Savior is a place where beauty resides. The section between His heart and yours is a clear whole piece of glass. It can be seen through, but it is solid without breakage of shard pieces. You can weigh it on a scale and discover the close-knit bond is strong with a glue that never deteriorates. God is the center, and you are the outer edge. Your importance to His being cannot be measured. There never will be a difficult encounter where God doesn't stand with you. He will carry the conversation or the workload, and He will dispel a broken word or misdirect. God cares about all people, and He grants favor to those who trust His direct lineage which implies He never fails. As is His way, He stands strong against adversity, and He punches with a fist of true endeavors, granting a person the opportunity to bring into his horizon, an exact replica of love and grace designed by the Master's hand. God never takes away a day's wage without first enabling the supplied plate of needed nourishment in the form of growth to the spirit. One may find starvation is a fact, but it is not because God hasn't offered true companionship at every turn of a man's thought process. Following wise counsel is a balance found by the individual who chooses to read the Word of God. This fact can't be denied but it can be proven. Watch a clown enact for the crowd. He is skillful in the entertainment industry, but can he dine on truth? Are his actions for pretend or is he simply living a life of falsehood? Many find God's Word to be a bore. That is because they don't realize the power therein. Should one need care or hope it is found between the pages of the leather-bound book or even the computer screen. God has made it possible for His truth to be told in many forms. This assures that no one can claim God did not reveal an opportunity to know Him better. Even those who never received a copy of the written scriptures have spiritually been offered to accept Jesus Christ. God operates in many realms. It is no different than a parent instructing a child to go to bed with an incentive of some form or another. The invite is what leads to the heart. Whether someone accepts this truth is entirely upon their own heart and mind. Some find faith and never leave it. The opportunity is what will be known come judgement hour. No one will be able to say they never heard God was real.

_____

_____

_____

_____

_____

The unknown way of a man is not by his design but by the Father's hand. God created a lineage for man to partake in the way of the cross. It is not for comfort or misdirect. It is for clarity, and an understanding which points to the true open door to God Himself.

Manufactured lies are just man's way of trying to control all factors for his gain regardless of whether another is injured in the process. If you follow a path that resembles this way of procuring your heart's desire, then you will fall victim to the falseness of love for Christ. Every person that thinks they have found grace because of the riches they have compiled is being deceived in the manner of faith. God does not offer wealth as a way to know Him better. It is simply due to a solid investment and a skilled way of mastering funds. Not all have the desire to gain wealth. Some prefer to know they have taken a measure of true devotion to either family or to other's welfare. You can build equity in many forms. Some require you to gamble on high stakes which may bring debt as well. If you take the approach that all money isn't equal, you will realize some of what you hold to your chest may be ill gotten or simply stolen from the hand of another. God does, however, build nest eggs and benefit the retirement plan in steps at a time. Wealth is lucrative. It is not pliable in the way a blessed soul can be. God counts wealth with a different measurement than man does. He holds the investment of a solid return as a gift of love in some form or another. If a caretaker were only interested in lining his pocket he wouldn't focus on the pain of the injured party, nor would he offer the best care possible. It is a heart thing where love is forefront, and it holds the attention of the person doing the work. All work holds benefits but some build retirements quicker than others. If someone guides with a settlement invested, they become a member who operates for the benefit of those he trusts and desires a plan of importance with. Not all will share their knowledge of status or ways to gain. Many feel they should be the one to offer gifts on their own terms. They don't want to invest so others grow. In the end many lose their acquired wealth to another because they fought so hard to hold it tight when, in reality, had they shared their knowledge many could have prospered. By God's design we are to offer guidance when we have gifts others can glean from. We are not alone, nor should we act as though we are. Don't wait until you have lost all your years before you decide to give. You will miss the joy, and the productive way others gain for themselves because you weren't generous. God watches and He invests in your spirit. You are safe when you return your investments back toward His direction. A bountiful harvest develops through the act of giving and it showers the mind with dignity.

_____

_____

_____

_____

_____

Teaching is significant to those who are in need of a ministry in which they learn a new field or graft of excellence. When you realize you can learn from another it opens a door to the unexplored opportunity in which the mind is entertained.

Make a plan and move toward the goal of obtaining what is needed for a completed origin of truth. This means one should always look at his skill level and build from there. If there are things you are in need of, practice learning what those gaps are that need filling and grow by way of education. If you think you have the needed requirements to proceed you may then enact with a new step forward toward the goal. Looking at the limits you possess gives clarity to the mind and determines how to proceed with caution, and an understanding of the needed elements to gain prosperity or riches of the material nature as well as the spiritual needs of the heart. A grown man gives truth when he decides God is who He serves. If a person enters into a contract where doubt is present, he is going to release a plan in which his back is covered. An area of study that produces a goldmine is the written Word of God. In the book He grafted to our hearts, are all the necessary features to gain a pure thought process along with a roadmap of how to live your life according to a true purpose designed by God's hand. We should all plan for the future, but we mustn't waste time only procuring a financial element to our accounts, we need to build for God Himself. That is when our hearts are happiest and our spirits content. Always looking to gain wealth leads one to the dark side of life in which no real gain is acquired that lasts a lifetime. If you are able you should strive to complete daily tasks that require work on the behalf of others as well as yourself. Showering others with gifts that speak to the heart is a design God favors for us all. The time frame of making a living is over the course of many years. In this process one gains insight in how to maneuver all gifts granted to him by God. Taking on a building process acts like a gateway to the future, but in reality, it is simply a formula to enhance our pocketbook, but through the endeavors one is enlightened to many facets of structure, which lead to the mechanism of growth and moral decision making. If you build with the hope of helping others, your heart will blossom and be true to the Savior. Looking at how you step forward each day, is a gift of enlightenment. You can see clearly when the vision is made crystal in the way of glass, in the sun with a beam running through it. If you haven't made the connection to this truth, you haven't reached the level of expertise that will bring success.

_____

_____

_____

_____

_____

_____

_____

People of mankind are not just looking for hope but a Savior who will help to lead them into the future with clarity as to who the Father is and how to serve Him.

The looking glass is not what people think. It is a time capsule in which the hour passes and the sand falls. It represents an hour's worth that is a simple reminder how time moves forward but doesn't escape the hour shaped body of glass. In the same manner a tale of excitement is shared then soon forgotten. Both have a meaning unique to one another, but both hold time as a value. God operates with a sound reasoning, and He is not one to forget who has served Him with their work. If you have built with a plan that is for His honor and His name, He will bring it about and create a place and setting where the ground is solid and true. He cares for those who enjoy His presence, and He invites the mind to call to Him in those situations. Building a structure can be daunting and a hard process to complete. A light from God giving direction can make the difference between a build ending in disaster or flames of life can be the result. Each thought for the better of man or God Himself will enact a close connection with the Savior which in turn develops His love and manifests it your direction. Giving a plan time to progress proves to be a wise endeavor. God is hospitable and He crafts with care. He does not rush through any job He is head of. Waiting brings into play a unique perspective that instructs the mind as to who is in control. God is the connection to the mind and in this embodiment two can become one. If you are trusting the lead of God, you will find time progresses smoothly and peace will be at your door. If you wait with the hope of a brighter day, then your thoughts are not in order. God wants us to live in the moment. He desires for our hearts to be content and for us to understand each motion from our bodies can be a gift to the spirit when we trust our actions are for the betterment of others and ourselves. A plan is often rushed and ruined because someone failed to give the time necessary for growth in one form or another. This can be said for the Leaning Tower of Pisa. Someone desired the build to be complete before it was ready and now it presents as a mistake for all to see. Even though it is recognized by the world is this a work of art or a mishappen tower of fun for the eye? It does not represent a well thought out design nor does it reflect care in the construction. Would you want this builder to design your home or office building? Forevermore this will be a witness as to the constructor's influence of failure. God constructs with wisdom and His plan is solid. He won't faulter or misstep. He will lead with grace and the right amount of character will shine through. You can trust His balance and His witness to your heart. Waiting is a gift to the heart. It can build a body of faith that will produce strength and a solid foundation for truth to rest upon.

Man does not see or hear the work of the Lord unless he engages with His spirit. This is done when one enters into a union of free will and hope toward the book of love. The Bible holds a gift that the heart can embrace and find truth. This guide is free to all man.

Today man is busy working and not looking at the Word God has to offer for him to learn and divulge truths. The written Gospel message is clear, and it portrays a line of hope that reaches the spirit and blesses the temple of man. God can distribute a pathway that will develop into a message of clear unity with His spirt. He does this when He approaches you with love and care. These are found from others who know Him personally. If you look at a family where God is center, they are bonded in Christ, and they are able to master a unity because they care and are guided with direction and purpose. All the work one offers to the Lord gifts them with enlightenment which provides a clear mentality of unity. Each plan that offers a motive of trust can demonstrate a connection in which a family bonds and grows together. All steps transcribe into a message of unity where trust is found and exhibited with no motive other than to see another accept the love of God. Each little endeavor brings about a motive that correlates into a gift in which the power of God is felt and accepted. God is directive and He never forces anyone to follow His direction. We reach a little higher when we engage and look at scripture. It is a message of hope that directs in truth with the name of Christ as its focal point. Christ alone guarantees the needed pathway where God Himself resides. Jesus is a caretaker. He is a delivery system in which man can form a bond with His spirt and be enlightened to who He is as a person. The cross was the mechanism in which blood was shed to receive man to the platform of grace. God's power rests in Jesus' arms alone. No one other than Christ can bring about a transformation within the heart or distribute truth to its core. The favor of the Lord is offered to anyone who trusts and accepts His salvation message. No other can bring about a plan that would match what God has done to precure His people to Himself. With Christ there is an open door you need only to walk through it. If doubt plagues your spirit look at scripture for strength. God offers faith by praying and leaning into Him through the process of acceptance for His Son, Jesus.

_____

_____

_____

_____

_____

_____

_____

_____

There is no witness greater than the one God has placed at the foot of the cross. The sacrifice of Jesus was a measure that had to be taken in order for man to gain understanding of the great love God has for His people. The blood had power that no man has. It belonged to the King, our God Jesus.

The template of Christ's body against the backdrop of two beams declares the sacrifice was pure and holy. Each drop contained in the veins of Christ is pure and red with justice. He is a Waymaker. He orchestrates and develops an outlet where people can gain a way to heaven. It is because of His love for them that they are able to engage with Him personally. He captures a life and sets it free. Only He can master this process. When man tries to gain entry to heaven's gate, he fails as he has no clear mentality to what must be done in order for such a thing to transpire. Thinking on your own involves a heart that is not pure or holy. For man has deception within him. God does not. He alone is the Master designer. He alone can produce a life and He alone can bring it to an end. Although man has a choice there is no real opportunity without the Lord. Even a small child can grasp the great promise Jesus provides. It is a simple yet complex undertaking. God's design is not weak nor is it without talent. He is a crafter on a scale that no man can compare. If you need to know how to find relief from your cares, read scripture and be given light. There is power in the word. Each syllable is unique but whole. It represents truth that cannot be compared. The Father's hand designed His Word to offer man strength. God knows the needs of man. He builds with precise commitment, and He doesn't fail. He never steps aside, nor does He venture out of range of the human heart. Every person is important and specific within the scope of God's love. Even this can't be controlled by anyone other than God Himself. God never accepts defeat. He will always be there in a time of need. He is available in the form of truth. His actions are pure, and they represent hope. He delivers a management tool of strength that never fails. How does He do this? Only God knows, but the power He holds is righteous. It contemplates the mind with wisdom and grafts the thought process to His personal style of thinking. When God is in control, He delivers a pattern of truth and dignity. God shows favor to a person when they accept His lead. Learning this function is a process where one is tied to the hand of leadership without being forced or manipulated.

_____

_____

_____

_____

_____

_____

_____

_____

Preaching is a gift many do not comprehend will grant favor to the spirit when it is heard. A sermon offers the truth of scripture when it is presented in a Godly manner. The Word, deciphered, grants the ear a home base and the spirit a resting place. All gifted speakers are blessed by the hand of God.

Dining on the Word from the Bible is a worship all its own. God watches and sees the way a heart responds to His truth. He knows when someone is engaged or becoming distracted, but even then, He directs the thoughts. If one trusts the process of the Word to their heart, they learn faster and absorb more hope the deeper they dive into the truth. An alignment takes shape where Christ is the caretaker and the individual, the body of His witness center. Each person who invests time with the Word never leaves in despair. The soul is rejuvenated, and wisdom is gained. A heart never presses the control button if it accepts the lead of its Master. God is not a tyrant. He is a leader with care who directs with purpose. His steps never lead in the wrong direction. He grants favor when the heart engages with His scripture. This process builds a bond and endorses the unique undertaking of unity created by the Master's hand. Looking to the future is not always wise if you only think on how to gain wealth and build more items of importance that hold no real value or weight of significance. The door to a kingdom has a latch way that only the master can control. The same can be said for those who trust only in themselves and don't serve the Lord who made them. God's kingdom can't be had by purchase with wealth. The only connection is through the saving grace offered from the death, burial and resurrection of King Jesus. He created the burden but also designed the mechanism to gain entry to His Lordship through the faith in His person. Look at what God has delivered through His Son and learn what real commitment looks like. No one, however how great, would offer as a sacrifice their kin so another could remain alive and well. This is how great the meaning of what God performed for His people is signified. People often wonder how could He have done such a thing? They don't realize the life it brought to all His children. Because of Christ's death all man could be saved. All people could know Him personally, and all could dwell with the Savior if they so choose. This is love represented in its purest form.

_____

_____

_____

_____

_____

_____

_____

Memories hold hope or despair. It is all about what you believe was true at the time. However, many fall prey to lies and are subject to doubt concerning their actions and their thoughts. God has the ability to relate the truth in such a way that you gain insight and a clear understanding of who you were at the time.

Traveling road shows bring into play a stage with simple construction. It is not made to host a large arena or gathering of the thousands. Anyone who understands the connection between multiples and many, has insight concerning size and build. If you are asking for the Lord to grant favor, remember He works in pairs. You and He are a unit. In the event work is underway within your spirit it may appear you are in a holding pattern. God works when all systems are a go, meaning you can't move forward if growth is needed in your life in some form or another. He builds character all the while He plants genuine heart goals that require a clear outlook and a desire for a mature representation in the work you do, and the efforts put forth must reflect a pure motive. Even then He may be building in some form that is not recognized by the mind. Just because things aren't moving where you presume, they should be is not a sign things are about to crumble. Each structure of good measure takes the appropriate amount of ingenuity designed by God Himself in order for success to be achieved. Take what you know and apply your heart toward a goal of goodness and things will develop when God directs the stage and the players align in the order of His command. Nothing is without fault in some form or another. God will right the way and lead with clarity, and He will build when the directive meets His perspective of good timing. God never faulters or loses step. He doesn't forget the forward motion and He builds with excellent character. He won't allow a path forward if the motion will bring hardship or decay in some form or another. He knows the best motive and faith is what draws Him near to a person. Look at how He developed the Word of God. It was manifested by more than one individual, by His hand alone, yet all the words are true and accurate. They hold power and they benefit the mind with clear incentives. There is no doubt or darkness within them. That is real concentration and instruction. The message is always powerful and beautiful with its intense lineage. God the Father has crafted well in the way of instruction. He is faithful and loving. By His grace we grow and learn through His gift of love we call home.

The screen before you when you read a written transcript does not read as power unlike the Word of God. It does not endow one with the gift of understanding nor does it frame a mind with endearments.

Stand at the gate of delivery by being close to Christ Himself. He is the Waymaker. None of your abilities can compare and your work is small next to Him. So, keep in mind working does not bring salvation to the heart. It simply attempts to appease the mind and fill it with duties that outlast a lifetime. Working is good, but it should not endow the mind at all times. If you have found a passion, make sure it doesn't override the love you have for your Savior. Looking like a master can bring fame that, too, is not life- giving. It is fleeting and frail with little endurance into the afterlife. Speak in clear messages when you lean into another but keep your focus on who delivers the true hope to a spirit. Trust the plan God has in place and let Him be the reason for growth. He can deliver you into a program that will enhance your stamina along with the goal of trust between you and Him. Be on the alert. Temptation can spring forth and drive a wedge between the work you enjoy and the Savior you follow. Taking goals to a level of hope which places them above the person of Christ, will bring a loss of communication and respect will be lost. God is revered and He enjoys a heart that is committed. If you find a stalemate in your progress rethink how you spend your time. Are you gaining in the ground of admiration for Jesus, or are you enamored within your own enjoyment of other things? Where do you place your time? Do you spend hours building for naught? Is the place of beauty you call home bound up in the circumstance of desire outside of perfection itself? Jesus is the only real thing that holds the heart of man whether he realizes it or not. The truth of a witness can be determined in the manner of connection. Do you pray and fast? Can a person see a commitment from the heart that bears a true pattern of hope brought about by faith and the expectation that God is real? Do you speak of the true identity you have found, or is Jesus on the back burner? If your focus is Christ, you will identify with His teachings, and they will be important in the work you do as well as the example you set before people you connect with. Christ is a God whose desire is to be first. He favors all. Look at how He provided food and security for the witnesses described as the Israelites. Even though they often were led astray He stayed faithful. That is who you serve.

_____

_____

_____

_____

_____

_____

_____

_____

People of today are not shy when they express themselves. There are social media and marketing features that sing of the truth. Look for strength by embracing what God has written. His people were true and fast in their presentation of His Word.

Today's marketing techniques bring about a pathway of hidden agendas. Man works to pay the bills; he favors his own wallet. In God's Word there is a divine gift from His spirt to the heart of man. There is no greater power one can own than a Bible and its many insights. If you engage and read, you will realize you have found the platform where a unity succumbs the mind and heart. This unity is a graft where God reaches to the heart of man and offers His love on every page. Explaining the way it offers love is expressed by the cross itself. Since God hung His Son on a beam and cross bar for the sake of man, His words are a guarantee as well. No doubt there is much to learn and glean from the practice of study. The needed material is supplied by many outlets so acquiring a copy is a simple matter. Deciding to enlarge your vocal reading offers a sound employment of instruction. The gate to knowledge is open when you do this practice. There are many passages explaining the love of Christ. Each one contains a memorable, visual tool for one's thoughts to relish the mental picture presented on the pages. The letters in red are exact accounts of Jesus, and His instructed material are written therein. Believe what is offered in the form of love and growth. Each message encompasses a thought process that develops the mind into clear recognition of the Almighty. God the Father is a caretaker and a human embodiment of a language only He can portray. His gift of language changes the mental endowment and brings light to the core so deception is removed and replaced with peace, a gift that can't be measured. Each passage contains a plan and a directive for the heart to reap the benefit and bloom into a being of clear mental transparency which dictates a love for one another. If you search the scriptures, you will find a passage that relates to you specifically for any given day. God speaks and brings about a love in which you grow with a mental aptitude to love beyond what man is capable of. God is the instrument that leads and benefits the soul with a gift of enlightenment where prosperity grows. How this happens depends on whether you have accepted the love offered. God does not push nor impose His own will. He simply offers a hand of recognition as to how to become a replica of the King by taking into account whom you serve. God and Jesus bring a lasting gateway that endures and teaches the mind how to act righteously with character and a true motive of ingenuity.

_____

_____

_____

_____

_____

_____

We build with strength and a purpose when God is at the helm of our business dealings. Counting the influence of the Maker as your individual desire, you can respond with a purposeful mental outlook.

The people who have taken it upon their mind and outlook to serve the King never lose footing or ground cover. Many know how to begin in faith and stay the course. Even when things are aligned or in their perfect order, delays can be a reality. God moves according to His timetable, and He never fails. If movement isn't happening, remember grace is sufficient in times of want. Be prosperous in thinking God has a plan, and He is able to bring about a course of action that develops with a precise momentum according to His will. If you tire of an act that is upon you, remember God builds in a direct manner. He never forgets and He never leaves a dream on the shelf that has been employed in a forward motion. A pattern of growth is at hand even when the light of instruction is standing still. Things need to flow and be specific to an outcome that brings beauty and a famed accord. God does not build junk nor waste a golden desire when it is true and purposeful. Each detail is an event, even if you can't see how it fits the puzzle just yet. All the work a build needs is often held in place over time. Growing procures an attitude of clarity that instructs and dashes the heart with a pure hope for a real and wholesome recognition in which God is honored. When you understand the Lord is the desired focal point, you will gain insight as to how to go about a directive where God is the ultimate builder. He is the one who crafts with care and makes a way. Things are brought about in an order that is clear. Never are there interruptions of dark interludes unless you yourself bring them in. God does not bring about an order where doubt is present, or where His presence can't be at home when the item is complete. God won't ever intrude upon a plan, but He can hinder the build if dark developments persist against His spirit. Thinking on how to gain fast returns can bring a plan of default. God won't operate in this realm. He favors a place of peace and harmony that is subject to the mentality of grace and a secure hope for forward motion in the form of love and opportunity. God delivers a dream once the decision is made for Him to do so. He does not graft a heart to desire something out of a dark premonition. This is not His way. If you build in faith, trust that He will acknowledge your goal and bring it into fruition. It may take awhile, but the balance of a true witness will be seen and developed with a clear reflection.

_____

_____

_____

_____

_____

_____

The foam of the ocean bubbles and breeds disease, yet it is able to support life. The fish dive and swim with grace and they breath freely with no ill effects. God manages the echo system and provides the needed elements for all detailed elements.

The tools one operates will enable him to build in a steadier manner. It will also ease his burden for the daily grind. The burden of a ministry is met when one enlists the power of God to enable him to build with care. The many facets involved may require more than a few adjustments on any given day. However, the more you grow in truth, the easier it will be to relate the message God has and to instruct His wisdom in a level of genuine intimate professions and maneuvers of grace. God offers a plan that is clear and precise. He will enact a forward motion in which there remains little doubt or confusion as to His calling in your life. When a visible opportunity comes into play, place your faith in His hands and He will grant favor. He will enable you to recognize the needed elements that will direct your footing and carry your thought process in the direction of growth. The plan will make sense and you will see a door that leads to a recognized outcome where faith is recognized as an element of true encouragement. The building process will be clear and there will be an element of courage graced with precise recognition that God is at work. You will have confidence with a measure of true purpose. The planning stage will be simple, but with clarity. The goal before you will not contain a burden too heavy to maneuver or operate through. God's grace will supply the needed steps and a passageway for them to be completed. The layout will reflect the hand of true guardianship and you will realize the arm of God is in control. The daily tasks will be revealed, and you will encounter growth with purpose. You won't find doubt a daunting measure nor will heartache ensue. With God the building process has purpose and comfort where His goodness is felt and embedded within your spirit. When you reflect on the time frame, you find a measure of grace has been upon you. The reflection will provide an aptitude that directs the mind according to His power and truth. God has been at work, and you will realize this measure as you sustain the direct purpose God has for you.

_____

_____

_____

_____

_____

_____

_____

_____

_____

Teaching is a requirement if God calls the heart to learn and gift others with instruction. You must gather a perspective of learning when truth is to be told. You can find faith in the pages of God's Word. It is clear and meaningful for all to learn and grow in a fashion of trust.

Teaching in a manner that allows for instruction is a gift offered from the hand of God. He favors the one who steps forth to tell His stories and His grace carries them far. Not all adhere to the boundaries, and they expand on the truth of God. This leads to an embankment of doubt and a frustrated body of followers. If a pardon is sought, the heart understands the beating of a man's character depends on whether he believes the Word of God to be true. If this is the case, you will find a fast atonement has developed and a clear network of the mind is seen. There will be no blank pages or misdirects, only a fast employment of unity with God's character. Being of a sound mind is an example of what is needed to graft a book or teach a tale of learning. God's character is on every page of written material produced by a faithful hand of study. If you look at how the universe was formed, you can grasp the longevity it holds in the form of greatness. Only God could master such a feat. Related material is found in manuscripts and panels of delegated hardware on the computer. Both serve a purpose and can eliminate the need for clutter, but the true source of education is obtained by applying the mind to the knowledge of who God is. With this enlightenment a gateway is given where a soul engages with the light of God. A pupil of study gains insight when the instructor knows His material with a thorough bond of intellect received as a result of applying action to growth. A manuscript is secure in the fact no other has written the exact same body of knowledge in the same manner. God does this to enlighten each individual according to their own learning style. People are made up of complex organisms. No two are exactly alike. They are separate but connected in the formation and design of the body.

However, a mind stands separate as well as the spirit. God has made man to be diverse. Our needs and wants may vary but in many forms, they are the same. Love is a mutual desire that all man holds within himself. If faith is present, the bounty of grace will be there as well. God has designed man to flourish in a structure of connected origin. He has not made him to stand alone. Crafting for the sake of love guarantees a growth style where home is the center and that represents the truth of who God is.

_____

_____

_____

_____

_____

_____

_____

Looking into the future with a hope for better employment often leads to a character where your present situation is lost in vision. Focus today on the fact God has provided you with an income. Place your trust in His person and prepare for more growth where God is in the lead.

Each step a person makes toward progress and a restitute outlook guarantees a faster progression in the way of progress and clarity. A statement in faith is the same as a witness of truth. Character is the basis for developmental progression where a standing and formal hope is projected. If one stands on truth he will flow into a river of desired meaning and the basis will hold fast. The projected outcome for an inspired plan is not to fail. Remembering that God controls all facets to all measures and decrees, brings a balance and an intake of mutual respect. If you fail to enlist the person of Christ, there will be misdirect and moments of failure will arise. Carefully judge who you follow. Is integrity part of the basic entities and are all people engaged in the manner of a correspondence where Christ is King? Many are led astray with the hope of pursuing a path that leads to fame or a gathering of income. Many lose their way out of greed and are subject to a negative employment. Christ evolves a pattern where faith meets a plan of organized dreams and endeavors which in turn treat each aspect of opportunity with a clear conscience. If you have found a dark thought enters the program, your building will have no character. Remove the burden when time permits and alleviate the structure of doubt. A glass ceiling will not carry the weight of many feet upon its threshold. Such is the case when a bottleneck design has implemented a hold on the structure you have implemented as a body of greatness. Look to Christ for leadership and a sound grasp of how to act. Don't let temptation rule your steps. Trust the grace God supplies and feel His person while you progress with a plan of integrity. Leadership is always based on the head crafter. The score of a game is the result of who ran the plays and how well they were implemented. A strong coach adheres to a guideline where his players can judge the outcome of his leadership. No one player is gifted so well that they hold the ball at all times. Many are needed to complete a play with success. These principles need implementation when considering how to manage any entity or structure of business.

_____

_____

_____

_____

_____

_____

_____

A commitment of truth is found by the hand that seeks the King and His ways. A tune of measure is calculated then understood in the way of excitement and honor that breaches the ground of intellect.

A unity found is what is known as a delivered gift from God. When you engage with His person you are granted an intellect that surpasses the norm. A field of enlightenment appears, and a recognition of trust takes place. A harbor of many ships does not release water when the boats are afloat. It waits until low tide to send them into the sea. The same principle is equated and thought through when objectivity is the goal. A unity with the King is a guarantee a person will thrive and deliver a plan that holds the mind at ease. If there are questions you have no answers to, rethink how the process began. Were steps taken that didn't follow the path of righteousness? Were you tempted then led astray hoping a right turn would correct itself? God is the trumpeter who engages with the sound of crisp enlightenment. Should the gate of doubt be present, where does your hope lie? God can correct any flaw or blend any gap, but first you need to acknowledge the cause for the dilemma. Many have found a path following true commitment comes from faith. If God is the deliverer, the plan will succeed. If you ventured into a swamp, let Him right the forefront and bequest to you a righted plan. Begin a tactic of clear direction. Seek God in the manner of prayer and a right thought process will return. Any ship has a rudder, and it steers a correct route when a map is in hand. The compass is a guide, and it keeps a balance between North and South. With God, this type of leading springs forth and a true platform begins to emerge. A tally of the day's workload is a good review when one's guidance as to how time has been spent is in question. This will keep a perspective concerning where application needs to be applied and where reprieve can take shape. Not all builds require a mass overload of workmanship to operate on a daily basis. Some require a weekly check to insure no deterioration has begun. In the event dust on the blinds of understanding sets in, question how your bank roll is dispersed. There may be a leakage that has sprung in the form of theft. An account of all monies should be calculated and tallied at the end of each pay period. If you alone manage your intake, recheck your tallys. It may be a simple computation that is in error.

An equal amount of gifts is grafted to all man. Some require different talents, but all are good and true. God grants man the ability to sing or to craft. He is the caretaker of both.

The balance beam holds the gymnast in a secure spot, however, one misstep and the balance is off. Should the footing be bad on a landing he will endanger his standing and eject a poor finish. Building a settlement where Christ is the lead brings into play a field of maneuverability encircling the mind with trust. The lead is satisfying to watch, and it brings the balance of a true craftsman to light. The sound of a machine worker is steady. The balance will be heard in the ear and a presentation of a true witness is seen by the strokes he applies with care. No person is without faults. It is how you go about correcting them that makes the difference. Always seek to reject a lie. You will escape much harm if you practice this type of mentality. A reflective mindset offers one the opportunity to guide in the way of an objective vision in which a sound practice can be relayed. Building a bond with God is a foundation where true magnetic relational origins transpire. You gain a path of fortitude and clear perspective. How this acquires the heart is a craft only God can distribute. When you feel overburdened take note of the hours you have placed upon yourself. Are you realistic with the expectation of your skill set or physical attributes? There needs to be balance between relaxation and physical labor whether that be in the form of study or application. Both require the effort of strength. Food intake should be wholesome with water at the forefront. God has given us much in the way of pleasure when we apply our skill set. You gain an appreciation of the mind and what it can do. With God in control, you recognize He is the giver and provider of all things good and true. If you are blessed to be a part of a body of believers, they too will stand out with talent that may be enhanced when a build is undertaken. If God has placed you on a lone mission, there will be others who come along side in areas where you can supply an outlet for their craft. No one is ever without the need for more labor at some point or another. Crafting is the plan for all men. God designs stairs in the form of opportunity, and we climb forward aiming toward the kingdom of life. This is found when we apply our mindset in His direction and calculate His guidance as our best asset.

_____

_____

_____

_____

_____

_____

_____

Today's market is slight for the man who desires a path of honest endeavors. One can find favor by multiplying the layers of true character against the backdrop of unity from God's Word.

Begin the process of unity by reading and applying the mindset of true hope toward the action of deliberate growth. Each undertaking is deliberate but necessary in order for a mature thought process to insure a solid bond and a reflective undertaking where Christ is King. Lead with character and growth sprouts wings. If one is to know the person of the Lord Himself, he must first believe Christ is his Savior. As a result of this belief a unity will develop where truth is recognized and fed, on a daily basis. You gain an upright individual hope when you accept the Word of God as righteous and dignified. Your heart will embrace the opinion that God alone is the creator and the majestic being described on the pages of truth. Each letter is right and just. There are no mistakes. Every word is a gift, and it supports the character found in the heart of God. You can find a path without Him, but it will lead to death. Walking outside of the Savior never results in a witness where faith is found. God is the founder and the maker of man's heart. He is the caretaker and the Waymaker. He grafts with precise applications, and He never leaves a person alone. He is faithful and true in all He does. God's grace is measured by His hand alone and applied by His command in an order in which no man can fathom. God builds and man learns to apply his skillset in the direction God directs. The heart is led, and it embraces the spirit of God when it seeks the path of righteousness. Only God can build in faith a true method of greatness. Only He can supply the needed material of importance in order for man to grow with clarity. During this process man can find a path forward if he so chooses. However, if doubt enters in, he may lose his way and become confused. Reading the Word of God brings with it a guidance manual that enlightens the mind with clear vision. You will gain in truth a connection to the most, high God and you will learn how to serve Him. Let Christ lead and be secure. He is the Waymaker and the path forward. When stepping forth toward a goal, engage in the format where unity guides the heart. God brings a clear understanding, and He lights the way. You will have hope where doubt used to reside. There will be grace and a light with inspiration at its core.

_____

_____

_____

_____

_____

_____

_____

Today's outlook of man shadows the King, but never gives light. Christ alone is the reason for hope. Only He can provide true nourishment for the mind and spirit.

Taking time to know the King is wise and measures truth. The format provided by the Word of God incorporates a wise counsel. Looking for hope, but never trusting what the Bible has to say, is a blind man's way of enlightenment. You see but you do not hear. The words of God's grace are many. You will understand the power they hold only if you bear witness to Jesus as Lord. You must first believe and accept that God is real. Only by His grace does enlightenment come. If a heart loves deception it won't find clear understanding. Only God is able to bring a soul to truth. Only He can offer the message of the cross. In this way a witness is known and seen. God's clarity is forthright with a perspective of clear vision. Gaining a true method of real hope, offers the mind a field of dreams. God's faith never fails. He offers a connection to His spirit, and He plans for the future. You will be guided with care and a measure of sure -footedness will evolve. Taking time to prepare a plan is wise in the eyes of all. With God, the measure you use will be a guide in the form of unity tied with trust. God does not deliver a false motive or a disconnect in the form of lies or deceit. You can trust His wise counsel. God will shower your mind with the needed requirements so your grasp will be solid and true. Walking in faith builds character. It grants favor in God's eyes, and He will embrace your faith with His own enlightenment. A skillset can be built upon only when God is at the helm. He crafts with pleasure, and He multiplies the good measure. God's witness is sure -footed. He balances each thought process and offers a way forward. With Christ you can progress and move with faith. God is a caretaker and a true partner. He plans with guidance, and He releases the power for you to gain in the way of a spiritual witness for His person. God directs with a clear and precise maneuver in which the spirit engages as well as the mind. His person edifies and He releases a true balance that creates an open pathway for the mind to follow. God is a true person. His workmanship is of a unique standing. He is delicate with a mature intellect. God is not selfish nor is He a tyrant. When a plan is presented, He will guide you through it.

_____

_____

_____

_____

_____

_____

_____

_____

People of today's generation are caught up and carried away by false opportunities. God is the Waymaker, and He provides the needed uplifting for all endeavors.

When God prepares a plan, it is forthright with balance and good measure. The seamline does not ravel, nor does it fray. The unity He brings is clear with order. God is a specialist, and He performs the necessary scriptural background that enhances His driven purpose. With Christ, one gains an intellect, and his witness is solid. The craftmanship is seen as complete and there are no tears or imperfections. The leading offered by His hand is grace and a connect of true identity. The plan will unfold with clear perception and a vital enhancement will be noted. God's plan will unfold, and wisdom will be recognized. There will be truth and a pattern of unity will be present. God does not over burden His pupil in the study of man-made material or engage him with a dark resolute. When a witness is seen or heard by man, his heart reacts in one form or another. He either accepts the truth, or rejects it as foolishness. The former will learn from this interaction and begin to study the resources available to him. God offers all the opportunity to know Him personally. A simple investment toward the purchase of a Bible will shower the mind with the gift of enlightenment when it is applied and read daily. This application guarantees the offering of a unified heart to Christ. The resource of the written Word is a tool that crafts with the design element of a unity bond. When a person recites the Word, He calls the spirit of God and invites Him to engage with him personally. This witness is recorded by the Father to His Son with the Lord's prayer. Grace is often heard when a prayer is recorded to God's heart. The act of fellowship with God is an undertaking by the union of one heart to another. All prayers are a witness that God alone can be visited and related to. By applying this application, you can gain an internal thought process which will guide you through the day. God favors a soul that is transparent. His workmanship can be seen on the hearts of man. Praying builds character. It supports the realization that God exists, and He is real. When you trust Him with your thoughts you express your faith in His person. God releases a maneuver in which a heart is bonded and supported to His frame by a thread of grace. This enactment allows man to know Him personally.

_____

_____

_____

_____

_____

_____

_____

The voice of man is shallow with little hope, but God serves man a delicacy of grace that only He can supply.

Today we witness the unity God offers through the manifestation of His Word to the mind where truth can be witnessed to. Managing the mind is a task enriched by the hand of God. He is the one who performs in the boundary of His love and grace. The backbone of grace is found when one applies his heart toward the growth of his person to Christ. Grace through prayer is a necessary measure which will allow the growth mechanism to be brought forward. Allowing Christ to lead will favor a heart with true understanding. Christ is the influence of truth. His character holds a place of recognition within the heart of man. God delivers unity and He crafts by way of understanding. He is a caretaker. His ambition is not slight but a source of true power. You can find strength at the altar of love known as the throne of God. God is a witness and truth can be found in Him. God's character is pure. It does not fall away but it enhances the mind with growth and showers it with truth. The power of grace is offered with love and true hope. Reading scripture will supply the mind with a true character witness. The work of the Father can be an instrument that directs the mind and leads it to truth. God the prophet of truth never fails nor goes a separate way. God walks with His people. He prepares them for growth with a loving hand. Grace is the manifestation of God's love. When it is applied the heart entangles the mind. The two are merged and a unity precedes. Another form of unity is realized when an admission of trust is understood. The action of prayer applied to the Savior's heart can be felt and administer a gateway from Him to you. Cleaving toward God's righteous hand, administers a profound pathway that incorporates a living well of faith. Living by way of faith is a bond of unity grafted by God's hand to the center of your being. Each step forward is a direct motive for you to engage and achieve personal growth in the direct connection from Christ to you. God is a manifester of truth. There is no doubt in His recognition. The power of grace is a measure that informs and delivers in depth a personified mental outlook in which Christ is center. God is a character of goodness and mercy. He has no flaws, and He is spiritual. God is the influence that one hears when He applies his heart toward the growth of insight. God manifests the mind, and He offers true guidance.

_____

_____

_____

_____

_____

_____

_____

The book of righteousness centers on truth. When followed, insight is formed within the mind and structure can be reasoned.

Timetables enhance the structure of a page with clear mental images to enlighten the mind with clear vision. Following the formula of a graph enables a person to visually grasp a time frame and its corresponding latitude of understanding. If a person builds with hope, he is joined in the spirit with Christ Himself. God offers His personal abilities toward the mind and enables a path of righteousness to occur. His behavior is a shadow which instills the mind with knowledge granted by His favor. God offers all mankind an opportunity to know Him better through the process of study. The application of His Word is joined by Him, and He wages a platform in which His person is known. God follows a measure of truth where He alone is the judge. His example is quality in its purest form. The structure of science teaches the mind how to maneuver the facts presented. God offers truth in the form of a union with His spirit. Teaching engulfs an attitude where the presented facts are comprehensible and straight forward. With God the spirit accepts His grace and the revelation that God holds the power of knowledge. A witness to this truth accepts the heart of God to Himself. In the process, a power is released and faith abounds. A clarity is received and viewed as a positive outlook. The truth of the Gospel is a powerful tool. One gains insight from its provision. The Word is infallible. God is the creator of all things good. His Word is an example of the power He holds. Trust in the leadership it offers. The book of truth is unity when applied and understood. God's grace will connect the spirit, and He will engage in the process of knowledge applied by way of His person. Learning to trust the King is a measure often restricted in the sense that man leans on himself for guidance. His focus is not correct, and he believes himself to control the things around him. With God, clarity is there and a focus of richness evolves. God is the center and with Him in control you gain a perspective of hope with pure intent. A focus of vitality is a witness that produces a clear authorship with a ground of good measure. The witness of man rests upon the hope that God is real. If you trust His character, then the Word of God presents as a plan of purity. Grace offers the mind a recluse way of connecting to the spirit of God. You can find hope in the pages God has provided. His plan is good and true.

Today we market ways to bring forth much in the way of material goods. With God, our hearts are built with a connection to His true character. Nothing compares by way of a true manifestation, of true wealth. God offers this.

The power of grace is an equal balance of true grit plus the endeavor of hope with a mature undertaking showing the power of love. When one applies a character witness, he soon realizes sin is not a part of the structure of goals. God supplies the mind with a craft and a learning in which opportunities abound. God is wholesome and fluent. He never tarries nor trespasses against the heart. He builds with character a true course of a gravitational pull that leads directly to His spirit. Should an individual leave the nest and begin a partnership with the Almighty, he will be granted favor as God responds to an outreach from His people. He posts a connected way of thinking, and it brings into play a grace in where all man can embrace the Son of Man. God is the supplier of many giftings. Recognizing the fact, He is the one who granted a man's holdings is expressed by the way one builds in faith. When God offers a person a way to connect with His spirit, He is extending hope in a war-torn world. Without God, no man can make right what is wrong. There is never a balance unless God delivers it. Truth is a manifest of the mind in which a secret way of ministry is achieved. How does this happen? God orchestrates the desired mental relationship goal with His own level character and a beauty of grace becomes comprehensible. Following a pattern of true love, all will know freedom when this is sought after. How does one go about gaining a true love of the Lord? He applies his actions in the form of reading the Word of God. He offers to Christ his spirit with a connection to the mindset that the Word of God is true. He believes and applies prayer in a forthright and determined mind set. He does not waiver on the fact that Christ alone is the Savior to mankind. With this thinking, a man will grow and learn in a fashion of grace alongside a field of recognition. All the hope one holds is a graft from God's spirit to the man's heart. God delivers a solid homeward bound cometic energy that salutes His person in the form of a religious guarantee that God is real. Only those who invest time with the Savior come to the throne with an abandonment. Without this application there can be no real complete unity. Prayer is the guideline that encapsules the thought process and delivers a true, relished mental way of thinking. The power of God is revealed, and you gain a grace that surpasses all.

_____

_____

_____

_____

_____

_____

_____

God is the true maker of all things good. He doesn't fail, and He never brings a plan of justice unless a crime has been committed. Stay true to the Word of God and you will go far.

If you're wondering how to transcribe a passage and there is not a grouping that applies to your way of thinking, remember Christ has a teaching tool that enlightens and draws Him close. He will gift you with a clear view and a way forward. You never take on a battle without first knowing where the plan will end. If defeat is on the horizon, change your strategy. You can do this by offering your dreams and goals to the King, Himself. He will listen and apply the needed measure once a true course of study has taken place. If you think you can work without guidance because you are a master of all, you have no real commitment to God. When you do apply your thoughts, He will enlarge the playing field and there will be clear vision. He crafts to bring to light the path forward. He is not about to bring hardship unless you have taken a wrong turn and are working outside of His direct course of action. God never loses the way, nor does He endanger a person's soul by being too strict. He calculates where and when a job should be done thus resulting in a solid adornment to move forward. Grace enters the scene when the mind can't comprehend how to step. With the focus in God's direction, you will find you have forgotten the negative pull and you will see the light. Truth is what God is about. He does not play games and He is not difficult to follow suit to. His plan will always breed a solid hope that carries the mind to a place of satisfaction. If you find you are always hoping for more, you have lost sight of what God is trying to do in your life. He leads and offers solid goals. He never steps away or moves out of sight. He is a good caretaker who can be trusted. God favors anyone willing to lead with a pure heart. Recognize this and be shielded from sin. Taking a step forward may be a frightening thought but serving the Lord in the process will make things clear. A focus on what God desires for you brings to light a certain gift that enhances the mindset that God's way is true. You can never go wrong when you let God lead. It is a fact that never fades. Construction begins when plans are developed. The blueprints act as a tool that supplies the legwork for a team of workers to go about their building process. No one builds alone. Others are always needed to assist in some form or another. God created us equal. We all share talent and craftmanship so engage in the process before you and let man be a part of the work you do.

_____

_____

_____

_____

_____

_____

_____

God's majestic line of truth is a witness that He is powerful and true. He never doubts or turns away. His grace is proven by the message of the cross.

When one travels, he finds many routes to take but the best one leads in a straight line unless tourism is the passion. God offers many opportunities to bask in the lane of true morality. If you care to know Him personally, make a map of how to get directly to Him. It is easy with an application of true unity when you seek His heart and hear His Word. Following along the path of least resistance, can bring about a formation where one is weak or alone in their pursuit. Traveling with the King requires a mindset that you must honor and entrust your person to Him alone. The caretaker of mankind knows how to blend the sea and the waves. He separates fresh water and conceals it in the globe. Know the Lord counteracts the dark thoughts that desire a home within your mind. If you pursue the real dominion of hope, you will find God at the heart of this endeavor. God is light. He can never be a dark spec or a lose cannon. He guides with a clear and purposeful way. Following the lead of the Master, offsets the guard of clarity and it speaks to the mind in a clear and adept way. Showering the mind with truth will lead in a clear undertaking that allows for growth in a personal way. The formation of truths gained by the knowledge of the Maker never leaves the heart. When you practice the principles outlined in the Word, a clear objective is gained. Many release their hold on their own insight and believe in the power God holds for them instead. A walkway never allows for more than a few feet in dimension if it is a sidewalk. Other paths may be large where many can pass. With God only one way is possible to know His person. Jesus is this connection. He is the Waymaker. With Him you can gain a sure- foothold that is unity at its finest. Don't expect man to provide what is out of his reach. Man cannot bridge the gap between himself and God. Only the Son is able to extend an open hand and bring about a life of hope toward a bond that lasts a lifetime, all through eternity. God's character is sound. He never drifts or steps outside of good measure. If you are banking on there being many ways to heaven, you are sadly mistaken. God's Word elaborates this fact on many occasions. Read the good book and be enlightened to its truth. Starting a bonfire will bring a roar from the crowd but it won't design a witness to the light it brings. It only supplies heat and a temporary burning of brightness. With God, there can never be a dark moment. He is eternal with light on His shoulders for all time. Capture the look of love and engage in the spirit of hope. Know God personally and you will be saved.

_____

_____

_____

_____

_____

_____

Teaching is a requirement for the experienced who desire to share knowledge. It comes in many forms, however, if God leads, we all learn.

The knowledge of good and evil is written between the many transcripts of the Word. There are many accounts of its teaching. When gaining insight, know the plan of truth is found with the witness God offers to His people. Only He is the one who can pave the mind with real integrity. He crafts with care and uploads a tablet with clear unity to His way of thinking. This takes place when someone engages with God's spirit and connects to Him. It is a gift God offers by way of unity with Him. He gauges just how to proceed when there is interest in who He really is. Time alone with the Savior brings into play moments of real decision making. His opportune management style is superior, and it provides a landline of true enterprise. Even when one is not in the construction business, God crafts with him to clarify how he should proceed. Be it a measure of hope for another, or a plan of riddance related to poor judgement, God always provides the necessary support and enables a thought process to unfold that will enrich and evolve with clear direct enactments. If you have understood God can provide a path forward, you know He will also build what is right and true. He will not take away a dark interlude. You must, yourself, commit to a solid way of presenting your material to others. Even when there is no bounty to be had a smooth transition can occur in the way of length in guidance or ministerial representation. Not all factions prove to be profitable. Some are designed to carry the mind to a brighter height where goodness and mercy flow. Work with the thought process that you are serving the King. In this manner you will come to see a saving mental reprieve. You won't be burdened with a mind that favors another life. This is dangerous and you will fall victim to a loss of good measure. Your actions will align only when Christ is center. Your hope will be fast and solid, and you will see a set standard develop that will carry you far. If a plan is not readily understood, think about why. Could there be a direct link to no growth as a result of no written material to follow? Do you need to develop the process and make it a new measure forward? If no guidance is available, trust your Savior to supply the standard you need. He is ever faithful with care of abundance. He won't leave you nor will He forsake your dreams and desires. He works with a careful measuring tool so grant Him time to complete what He has underway. Your timetable is separate from His. His will is always better. Give Him the recognition He deserves and know His person better. It will ease the time frame of waiting.

Tonight, the wind will howl and blow. With it will be the pleasure of a solid waterfall from the skies above. Rain brings a balance to the earth and the ground receives a dose of nourishment.

The plan of God is always good measure. Every opportunity He provides is calculated and true. He does not advance in the form of a negative marker or ground material in which dirt clouds the judgment. His voice is steady and sure. It reflects a mountain of true inspiration. There will always be room for growth, and you will see a clear mental outlook that provides hope with a dash of understanding. God builds in stages. He crafts with care, and He reflects His person to the organized process to enhance the pattern of truth in each step. When a loss is embedded, the article affected may have been tarnished. There may have been a need for more intellect or study before moving forward. God inspires the mind with crafting, and He holds fast to the table of true character. Being part of the body supports the groundwork that man has a caregiver and a friend for all time. Jesus views love as the main embodiment. If you follow the lead of a witness that is true, your intellect will develop a grounded maternal advancement and there will be a light provided. The care you offer another supports your belief God is real. When you turn your back and admonish pain you are acting out of evil. A plan will unfold but it may not support your needs and it will separate the love of God from your person. A gift of the spirit is never something that brings evil into play. It will direct in a smooth and forthright manner. You will align the understanding of the Word of God with your motives and you will then recognize a true kinship with the Master. All the true motives shine with a reflective seal seen by other representatives of the cross. If a heart slips into a forward motion of negative articles or embellishments, it will fail to see the lifeline God offers, or simply put, the judgment becomes clouded. Take what you know from the Word of God and let that be your guide. Show favor to those less fortunate and consider the way you desire someone to see you as a person. If care is needed, and none is available, offer a helping hand and be the reason someone succeeds. It may be a small offering or perhaps one of a dignified undertaking. Either way, God will see and approve of your set of gifts being shared with someone less fortunate.

_____

_____

_____

_____

_____

_____

_____

The power of the cross is seen as a true connection of the spirit in the form of grace. If you believe God favors His Son, know He loves all who turn to His person.

When seeking to know the King, engage with Him in the form of reading the witness material He offers daily. It is crafted with the hope one needs to gain understanding that God is real. The power within the pages is brilliant and true. Each little detail transcribes the heart and makes it whole. It does this by the hand of God pressed into the spirit of your will. God does not force His way into your consciousness. He suggests how to know Him and brings a beauty where you learn who He is and how to please Him. He is not a tyrant. He is a caretaker where He always leads with true character. He lets man decide for himself who to follow. If God is your Master, then you have realized the power of true kinship with the great I Am. God the Father is designed in such a way that none can compare. How He was made we do not know. He is a being that has no beginning or end. The sacrifice God offered, in the form of justice, for man to be able to meet with His person, and know Him personally, is an example of His great love. He alone was able to build a bridge that constructed the needed measure for grace to adhere a purposeful bounty with care at its core. Only God could bring about such a gift. He gave Himself so that we may live, such a gift of latitude and monetary gain in the form of true personal commitment. No one loves as much as Christ, the great I Am. He builds in such a way that the heart is always set free against a backdrop of immaterial doubt and a claim of indignity. The witness portrayed is accurate and is reflective to those who have gained a unity with the King. They know Him personally and they engage with His character. The written Word formulates a hope that burnishes the mind and grafts it to His mental outlook. With God all things are made clear. If confusion is present, reflect on the source that gained entry to your thinking process. How did it come about? Were you enticed by the dollar or the dream of many riches? Were you thinking your plan was solid because it offered great wealth? This is not the way Christ builds character. He designs a manufactured mental and physical calm that realizes man needs more than personal wealth. The desire of man is truly to know God, the Father, more than Himself. This produces a wholesome way of life. If you desire things outside of faith and love, you have not understood the way God operates or His goals for your life. Reflect on who you want to be and consider how God would view your thoughts. This is how you gain personal commitment and a true hope for the everlasting.

Build with character and you realize grace is a beautiful thing. The hope you will find will be fruitful and full of love.

Today we find the marker of history being removed. Many have followed the path of least resistance and fallen prey to the dark one. When a person hits rock bottom they embrace a lie hoping it will bring light. When the realization that the true King of this world is the Waymaker you gain insight, and a map of clarity is revealed. If you raise up truth in a common practice of your daily walk, all knowledge becomes clear. The realization that you hold the key to a meaningful and prosperous life is apparent. Looking outside of the law of man and looking toward the true connected Savior, a reality that is born with a message of guidance and is relevant. Otherwise, a mere existence is what takes place. Thriving in life is not found in what your bank account holds. It is the realization that there is a true God, that He exists and that He is powerful. No other can compete. God formulates the plan of life with a character full of opportune movements in which time is a factor by way of growth. If you follow hoping to bend the bar, you will find a tangled web of deceit. You may gain in monetary ways, but your heart will harden, and you will be lost. The character you portray will be clear to others and there will be no grace offered on judgment day. You can argue or hope for a reprieve, but how you spend your wealth here on earth is determined and measured against your actions and how they related to others and their good will. If you cheat and abhor the truth of God's Word and you look outside of it, you will gain a long history of doubt and a dark presence will ensue. You will be controlled by its power, and you will lose faith without truly gaining the wisdom offered by the leadership of God, the Father. If one delivers a false brand, he is enticed to continue the practice. There is one simple way to know God is your hindsight. If you care more about how to gain wealth or fame than you do His connection to you personally, you will exist in a lie. There will only be a lead of contempt the more you engage in the practice. If you are clear in your desire to know judgment by the hand of God, and you relish His objective insight, then you are embracing the way of the King. God will never offer great returns in a dangerous manner. Nor will He object if you pursue His heart. He will grant a limited amount of doubt, but in the big picture, you will have to believe upon Him, or you will lose focus. If you waiver and walk on the line, that is the same as a rejection of His person.

_____

_____

_____

_____

_____

_____

_____

_____

A second of time is calculated by the hand of the Almighty. He never fails or breaks a promise. His words are true, and He is secure in and of Himself.

A talking point of faith will provide a thought in which the mind gathers a plan of action. All God offers, He will supply if a spirit believes He is King. Your mind and soul are a team and they both need to connect with the fact the Lord is who balances the equation. God is the source of a true design that enhances the ability to graft right and true behavior. Following in the manner of good character you will find a path that leads to a field of good measure. You will learn that a short cut can bring only a departure from the real goal and that is to secure a place with the Savior upon death. When you follow the crowd, you will lose face in the backdrop of lies they offer the mind. Standing in the way of prosperity comes by way of true kinship with the one known as Lord. Our God does not bring to the playing field a maneuver of personal investment. For He cannot be improved upon. God can't be outdone. No one person ever gets past the throne as there is no entry found beyond that which God has put in place for us to discover. Following Him in faith is a sure manual means of gaining a clear noted transcript in which He manifests His love and covers you in grace. Looking toward a home, brings the mind a safe place to rest unless an outside force brings darkness and harm. With God home is found in His arms of comfort. He alone is the one who carries the mind into clear forests. Even the dark leaves of green balance the blue of the skies. God has developed a plan for man to know Him personally. This is represented in the manner of true companionship offered in the form of blood upon the cross. The bleeding that took place was a measure that offered our redemptive account against the lie of Satan who testified that man was fallen. God redeemed man by way of His Son so no longer must we live in shame. Our sinful nature is imperfect, but the grace of God reassures our steps become part of His demeanor. This is a result of His care, and His able bodied definement of our heart. Should one escape the wrath of God, it will simply be because God provided the way. The shoulder of responsibility is truly ours alone. It is our choice that brings life or death. The open door is available. Whether a person decides to claim its existence is purely of his own knowledge and accepted witness. Trust in the Savior and gain a life of long standing. Eternity will never fade, and the bridge of sacrifice is clear. Take God's hand and know Him for real by way of the message of truth found at the foot of the cross. The hour is short. Accept him now or fade into the sunset with no true measure of life ever after. Hell is real and the flames are hot. What awaits your future depends on you.

_____

_____

_____

_____

_____

Trust is gained when one is true and faithful. When a direct path of dark unfolds people walk to the other side hoping for relief. When blindness sets in a plan of deception is produced. Learn truth and know how to stand firm against sin and debauchery.

The power found with grace breeds a true encampment of the heart and mind. All the people who have engaged with Christ learn there is hope for their days ahead. Time, they relinquish to His hand alone, and they offer themselves as a witness for others to learn the true nature of God above. No one is without fault but those who practice it are only kidding themselves that they can bear witness for Christ. If you practice deception and are untrue in character, you will lose the ground ministry God has laid out before you. All of man is to direct his faith in the right direction, otherwise it is a false representation with no real purpose. The caretaking God offers is right and true. He is a Planner and a Waymaker. No one person has the ability to build as the Savior does. No one can implement a solid standing where no doubt or deception enters in. With God the plan will always be recognized as good and sure. If you're feeling a little heavy, reach toward the table of true honorship. That is Christ alone. He stands true and resourceful always knowing which way to turn. God can offer any individual a reprieve against the black sky that hovers about. He does this in the way of the power He holds. Satan's objective is to destroy. He will never grant peace so enlist your thought process in a guarded manner always relying on the power God holds as your command. God will supply the necessary bond and produce for you a pattern of divine inspiration. You will then move toward the light and be refreshed. God doesn't just elect people with many talents or much charisma. He brings to the cross the broken and the dejected. Those who need Him most. He recognizes their cry because it is meaningful and true. A false "hail Mary" will not bring to life a heart by God's design. He knows the real character and He works with those who are truthful. You can't get away with sneaky embarkments, and you won't find faith a tool if the offering you give is a direct violation of a pure request or motive. God entangles those who are true and who are willing to learn and grow. Each step forward is direct with grace and a balance of love coming from within. It is not gained by advances of adultery or arrogance. God loves those who treasure His person. The people He grafts Himself to are genuine in their care for Him. They don't cheat or lie, and they search His Word for enlightenment. If you favor time with Christ, your heart calls to Him and He receives what you offer with an aptitude of endearment.

_____

_____

_____

_____

_____

Today is bright but not in the way of the sun. The true connected spirit is granted when one favors the way of the Lord. Character is achieved with the building of true moral ground and height.

The study of God's will is not always applied in the way one perceives. An echo of truth will sound when a plan is ready and in the right time zone. Meaning all the work and labor have met and are stationed on the horizon of beauty where the plan is seen as righteous. If you have built but no opportunity is available to go forward, wait until God reveals the masterful ordained way that speaks of unity, and a clear witness will be revealed. If you feel pressured and unsure, but forcing the fact that you think you should be moving for the sake of a witness, know God may have another motive for the stay. You could be a fraction away from grace in the way He processes your platform or guardianship of the mind. Stepping into a trap is not always apparent until it happens. God the Father is clear with a seen intent that all factions represent a precise undertaking that brings glory and a manifested mindset. If you feel left in the cold with little to show for what you have gathered or procured, you aren't understanding God is a Witness Maker. He may be revealing something in a form of gratitude that enhances the mind with trust and a true kinship with Him personally. God knows the heart and He builds a plan that suits that individual. He won't ask you to do something that brings you a downtrodden mental view of Him. If you think you should accept defeat and relate to a simpler gain, that is not the God the Word speaks of. He crafts, with care and a diligent mental view that brings about a gain of wealth not only in the material sense, but a spiritual gain is realized, one that only He could provide. He knows all the details of every mind and He divulges insight when it is needed. He won't make you do a job that interferes with His grace or His outlook of love. Would a father give a child clay when he desired a wood frame for his bed? Would rest come if he did? The God of the Word tells many reasons why He is able to perform the needed gain and interest for a job and He accepts His responsibility as the provider. He enjoys offering to His children golden motives and sure, plans of mercy. He crafts the heart in such a way that it receives instruction with guidance and love. He is a ritual of purity. His love is grand and whole. Embrace Him and know He will never fail you.

_____

_____

_____

_____

_____

_____

_____

God's gift is a pleasure mine of truth and opportunity. He is a Waymaker and a true friend.

Following in the way of love is a saving way to think. It speaks of a unity in which the Savior is the objective, and His viewpoint matters to you. If you gain wealth but have no track record for doing good through the process of which you acquired it, there is no representation of an honest barter or ground material of stamina. Easy gain can be had, but the formula for it never bodes well. If you share your goods, but have no connection to the people you gift, where is the purpose in the action itself? God alone is the seen administrator for man. He is the reason one should divulge and offer true management for any searching for a better way. The long-term goal of a witness is to stay the course and build in faith. God allows each individual to represent Him if they so choose. How one offers this function is representative as to his true character and motive. Allowing others to glean a reputation of honest merit, but never really engaging in the process that builds a plan to fruition, does not allow for grace to be submitted. A caretaker, such as God, always allows for the lost to gain knowledge in a place of true recognized endearment, meaning you can build but how you trust the Lord is what determines whether you have done well or if you just coasted through the time frame and prospered simply as a means to become wealthy. Working toward a career can be diligent work. Some find this rewarding while others pursue a life of living on the edge. Caretaking is a sound way to develop a pattern of faith. It allows for a person to gain both financial interests alongside the benefit of spiritual witness and true character. But it must be done with love at its core. If you enjoy the young, a life of coaching or spiritual guidance in the form of benefactor can bring mental enjoyment and hope to many. Remember, not all think a life of luxury is for them. Some enjoy the physical gain of endurance in the form of manual labor. Both serve in a manner that is right and true. If you enjoy working with your hands, you may be a crafter or an agent of a skill set requiring the eye of construction as a goal. Don't ridicule another's profession simply because it does not construe to your liking. There are many benefits to doing a job well done and enjoying the process, as opposed to a life of gain with no purpose or enjoyment as you work. Look at the profession of ministry, there is little recognition or fame, yet the heart feels secure and motivated in the belief that God has guided them into a job of good measure.

_____

_____

_____

_____

_____

_____

_____

_____

Thinking on your own delivers a faith that is shallow. With God the fulfilling gift of love is graced in the spirit, and it unites in the heart and mind.

Be proud of the work you are doing, but do not overthink your value. Realize God is the one to deliver your good measure. He graces the mind, and He develops the true witness of any person who engages with Him in a spiritual manner. If you seek only to gain material wealth, you will find, at the door of death a shallow life has brought you the grave of death with no hope of a good spiritual connection to Christ. As a result, you will not gain entry to the door of heaven. You will rest in darkness for all time. Many desire to know the gain of employment, yet they don't gain a measure of good material wealth. The problem with always seeking after monetary means is one day it will all rust and decay or another will benefit from what you have toiled your life for. Plant good seeds of unity and solid factions of importance that are described by the Word of God. If shelter is not found by the body, it will perish so is the balance of all man if he never trusts in the King and Savior. Jesus is the Waymaker. He is what man strives to be known by. Even if a person does not believe, it is written upon his character who Jesus truly is. All of man accepts a higher power, but whom they trust with their personal mental mindset and spirit, is who they will follow. The enemy offers pain and anguish though he is not honest about it. He will deceive one into thinking he will always supply sure -footing in a life, but this is false representation at its finest. All the enemy of God is truly known for is how he bore false witness in the garden of Eden. That was the first encounter where he showed his true make up. Learn from the story and know Satan is a murderer. Because of him all of man must suffer and toil on this earth. Had man not succumbed to the temptation of the devil, he would today rest with Jesus and know Him as Lord without the dire responsibility of working for all he owns. God would have showered each person with the opportunity to be responsible, yet free to roam and garden with ease. Each profession has gleaned from another's perspective along the way. God is the one who benefited the individual and led him to a stronger way of thinking. Today we work and pray for a more substantial home life. This is the case when one trusts the Savior and allows Him to work within his being. We grow as a result and our intellect is solid. With God we are not daft or deprived. We are peace seekers and true companions in which the Lord manifests His true desires. When a plan is understood in its completeness our minds relax and shine with true character.

_____

_____

_____

_____

_____

_____

_____

There is light with a bounty of giving truth if one listens to the Word of the Lord. All God offers is found in its pages.

Being of the faith does not require a landmine of guilt or persuasion resulting in no clear path forward. Instead, it offers a united lead of direct ministerial operatives that gain a man a disposition of real character. Growing in the way of unity is not often gleaned or represented the way one would think. With gifts of the spirit, a person is led to a ministry whether he preaches or teaches the Word in another form. Many times, you can't comprehend the need until God reveals it to you. People often work in a field thinking they have been required to. Not the case if a shadow of light reveals the real meaning to your clarified body of grace. You have honor and grace when you work for the Lord whether it be mopping floors or reading material related to growing a business. All can be done in a manner that is pleasing to Christ and His Father. If you think all you do is not material related to serving, perhaps your eye is searching for something outside of true character or enhancement of the mind. Little acts of kindness are true measures of a person's real state of mind or his developmental outlook toward God alone. Gathering a bounty can bring with it much in the way of returns, but have you thought about the way it measures up to what God would reflect as pure? Should you be devasted or left with no hope where would you turn? Do you think you can do all and maintain a crowd forever? Are you the king in your own eyes? If this is the case, you have not understood who the God of the universe really is. You haven't gleaned an adept mental gain that incorporates the real meaning of any venture. God alone represents true character. He alone measures the heart of a man. Only He is the way when it comes to a formal unity of the mind. Without knowing where to turn what does one do? How you perceive God to be is not the real answer. Who God is can be found only in the pages He has prepared. Written material describing Him must follow suit with the record of valor He, Himself, displayed in His heavenly host of words. God does not follow man. He leads Him into a clear field of unity with His spirit. All gates are closed that lead to any other value of gifted greatness. There is only deception from one to another if God has not led the way or offered His personal take on things. God the Father is the reason man has any hope of life. It was His great offering that enhanced the ability for anyone to live with a true hope forever after. God is the provider, and He will offer all the same chance at life with Him.

_____

_____

_____

_____

_____

_____

_____

Taking on the time of a challenge can be a difficult yet rewarding feat. God offers assistance when you apply yourself to His person and bask on His grace.

Time is understood as beneficial when one gleans the outlook that God is in control. He will formulate the path forward and you will comprehend how to go forward even when doubt is at the door. God removes the trespass, and a clear shield guards the mind. The bounty of a graft with the King is His measure of truth He will display when He deems the time is correct for growth. A shadow may be present so wait until you have understood the detail that makes it a cloud. Once that has been determined, going the extra mile will come as a breeze instead of a wind. You won't feel as though you have had to participate in a whirlwind, but a paced race in which you covered the miles with fuel and a tank of opportunity. All God offers is just. Remember He does not lead astray, nor would He ask you to go against His teaching of true moral righteousness. God upholds His own factions, and He displays them while you progress forward to the finish line. If ever you doubt you are to proceed, consider the reason you hesitate. Is it due to a malware within your computer sight meaning there is a corrupt plan in the making? Are you led in a true manner or are you forcing your will into the situation? When tackling the bones of a structure the foundation must be a permanent part of the constructed project. It cannot be replaced later. This is how our measure of work must be accomplished. Each step needs a line in the sand where the mind looks at what is taking place and it forms to the true character of what God would display. If you're struggling and have not found the open door of relief, wait and see how the future might bring into play another angle or opportune ministry of good fruit. Many times, people go forward in hopes of offering a new option just because the wait has proven difficult. Time is a factor we need to adhere to when God is in control. Jumping forward brings with it a delay in the result of a redo. Never bargain against the percent of a realized motive of good measure. God will work and prove it true. If the bounty outweighs the purpose, you will see a false exhibit revealed. It won't carry the sound of truth, nor will it be blessed from God's hand. If you struggle in the way of a unified outlook, you haven't found the connection between faith and the King. Jesus is a unified worker. He and the Father build as one. He never steps alone or without scriptural guidance. God relates to those who do the same.

———————————————————————————

———————————————————————————

———————————————————————————

———————————————————————————

———————————————————————————

———————————————————————————

———————————————————————————

———————————————————————————

The price of a debt against a man is not seen as a means but a detriment. If you bank on a finance of little material wealth but a holding of true character, the moment you arrive to a blend of sanctity you will harvest a true battle of wills.

The management of a corporation is a true skill set. Anyone who invests in the education along with the goal of a true enforced mental stamina which enables the mind to operate the relational undertaking of a mental witness where the practice brings about a true form of grit. Teaching the Word of the Lord is a spiritual maneuver where man invests in the opportune element of a study designed for him to retain the important realization that God is the one who directs the plan and makes it grow. A harvest is had in both scenarios but the one of fruit carries the heart and mind to a local community where God is the intentional inspiration and true builder of faith. You can't create a bond by only seeking a greater income. Traditionalists sink their teeth into a plan that offers a way to blend time and management skills into a table of divine character. If you recognize God is the one who invests the mind with true responsible integral thought processes, then you see He has gifted a unique responsible plan where His character is reflected in you. Looking to manage a build of an extent design can only be accomplished when His hand is applied, and He determines how the progress moves in any direct course. God will grant favor to a person when they have clearly decided He is the Waymaker. He has the ability to define a plan and bring about riches, but He never harms another in the process. He invests His great work and leads with a clear mental trace that is enriched by the power He portrays. If you consult His Word, you will gain a perspective that only He can provide. He will clear your mind and bring you to the plan of great integrity. He will bolster your aptitude and deliver your mindset to a clear hope that He will provide your means and needed expenses will be covered. God cares for all man, and He works for their favor. He shoulders the minimum expense as well as the grand amount of the total contribution it takes to end with a budget that is clear and precise. No gap will be present, and no leach of true goodness will fall short. The plan will be right and true and there will exist a way forward for more growth. Even when times are tough, God reveals how to gain more in the way of bounty. If starvation is on the platform, He will provide food and you will be nourished. People who trust His leadership learn He cares, and He is a multiplier of great inheritance.

_____

_____

_____

_____

_____

_____

_____

_____

Calculating how to perform a master plan is not always an accurate mental guess or laid out trilogy. The plan is a material opportune look at what needs to transpire and be performed. God is the head, and He grants knowledge to anyone who trusts His person. Crafting without Him is a foolish way to pursue a dream.

Man holds a heart in the mind and looks at the will of God as His lead and mainstay. God does not loom over His workers nor put them in a place of hardship or loss. He grants favor and He leads with a solid opportune mental picture where profit and gain can be had. A material opportune gift can be granted and harvested if love is at its core. If you gain outside of marriage to the great Almighty you will not be committed nor will you honor His intent in your life. A balance of quick magnitude results in a plan of deceit and no one rewards a misshapen work of art. It must present as true and in place with flare that encompasses the out lay that is to be witnessed upon. Going against the norm is not always bad. However, if you faulter, you will be considered a fool. But in the event you bring forth much gain you will be recognized as a true martyr and you will lead others to a goal of mixed elements that shed light on the craft you have perfected. Looking at what lays before you and realizing you need another to help in the endeavor is wise counsel. Plans never formulate without first being pressed upon the mind from God's hand. In the event the plan is dark it was not gifted by the true King. If it is a reflective cast of great understudy where truth can be witnessed and understood, then you can be assured by the moral character that all is well. God does not turn away from an endeavor in which His person is reflected in a positive and holy situational verdict. God will restore a person if his person is true and of good character so all may gain true growth and a reward of great inheritance. Building in the way God provides is a motive to do well. He will always give the best understood way of going about any opportune advancement. He does not strike out against someone when they are working to secure a plan of importance that celebrates the way God is reflected in the Word He offers through His encampment of the pages of life.

_____

_____

_____

_____

_____

_____

_____

_____

_____

When one looks out a window, he sees the street and lights in the sky. He gains a look into the realm of a day's work by witnessing the cars go by. God alone is the one who crafts each person and leads them to clarity and focus for a day's work or leisure.

A badge of honor is a gift from man when a job is completed, and the plan is made whole. With God, we see a plan and know He is the one who crafted it. He made a way for the light to shine and clarity to be revealed. He built within our thought process a vision and a true element in where we focus toward His person. When we follow the path God lays before our hearts, we glean in a way no other can present. Only God can deliver a technique in which all details are made wholesome and pure. With His way in our mindset, we endeavor forward into the path of righteous mental servitude. Our Father is a crafter who never leaves the bounty on the shelf. He makes a moment where we glean a close unity with Him, and we desire more of His greatness. If a person has completed a major endeavor and has had success at his backside, he accepts the gain as a good investment of his pursuits. All the while decisions have been made that reflect as to whether he serves the King or himself. God does not pursue a path where negative dark forces are present. You can't witness the light if you invite the dark before each step. Remember God is always a force of true light and a reflective stature of goodness and mercy. He will not attempt to gain a person wealth when he knows it will destroy him. If you desire great wealth, you are not focusing on where the true treasure and reward are to life eternal. The plan of a good engineer never has holes that can't be filled with good, rich material. Following toward the goal of true connective enlightenment is a lead only God can provide. He will speak with a connective spirit, and you will hear His clear directive which will prosper you in the way of quality, productive heritage. No one desires a worker who never offers up hope or integral true motives in their display of progressive movements. If you labor just for the gains, your heart will embark on all thoughts of ill repute. You will balance your spirit if you look at how the Savior has offered grace in the way of the cross. His gift to man was precious and it delivered a bond in which none can severe the cord or break its hold on the spirit. If you have linked your mindset with God, there is no leak or dismantled leg work being done. A true connective design is underway. It may take time, but growth will be apparent during the process.

There is a missile that pulses with a purpose to destroy yet it may miss its target and fall short resulting in no bounty for the team who sent it sailing. God does not miss the mark of any target He sets His sights on.

God can formulate a build and develop it into a solid masterpiece with a functional display of perfect order. If you wonder what steps to carry forward have you considered what the outcome will be? The design factor may have a glitch, or it may reflect poor judgement in the form of no real function. Do you desire a quaint, but purposeful outcome, or are your dreams of a grand scale? Both have merit and should be considered before you engage in the function of a strategic harvest. A plan with loopholes may lead to a clear number of distinct negatives where no real effort can be achieved. You must engage with hope of a true commitment in which a part is released that holds the doubt. All negative influences should be removed before you administer your duty task. All on board with the build need to realize their part in an intricate detail only they have knowledge to. All crafters are special in that each holds the skillset and the mindset of how to achieve the desired affect for each element they hold the responsibility for. No one is to blame when a natural disaster happens, but if one intentionally sets fire to the production by procrastinating or purposefully doing shoddy work, they are not a team player nor will they achieve much in the way of a heavenly bounty from God above. All the result of any endeavor is the related efforts of each person who played a role in the building process. Many feel entitled to claim for themselves some of the gifted talents that others performed. This is a false representation of true character. If you freely express who the beneficiaries should be concerning who performed the work, you reflect well upon yourself in the process. People understand there is never just one side to a story. Two influences have taken part in the maturing of a marriage. Ground is covered when one enlists the partner to share in the responsibility alongside the riches gained thus resulting in a solid unity between the two. If one partner reflects poorly, the other will see this as a slain momentum and he too will step aside in a manner of lost productivity. The marriage will fail, and a bond will break. God will deliver reconciliation only when repentance is undertaken, and a way forward is met. He does not set aside a dark unity just for the sake of partnership. You must be honest and fair if you expect a solid bond in any form where others are involved. Walking away from a union destroys a witness and it tears apart the longevity you sought after.

_____

_____

_____

_____

_____

_____

_____

The steeple of a church is brilliant in its design. It reflects a character of hope all the while portraying a unity with the crafted walls and building structure. God creates beauty with a flare and talent none can compare to.

The sidewalls of a studded tire wear down with the road under their bearings. No two tires wear the same. Each has a separate but distinct measure of rubber around the rim. God designs with the element of uniqueness as well. He is the one who designed the road and brought the rubber into the tire formation. He is a caretaker who divulges a mass undertaking with each display of the sky setting at night. No one individual bounty of harvest ever measures the same. God calculates each grain and puts it in the bin for sale at a later date. Saving represents a character where supplemental income returns good favor in the form of wealth to the account of understanding. If you harvest with the intent of selling all you have brought forth, you may find no funds available at the end of the year. A good manager realizes he needs to balance the account with debits and credits. One month may show a reflection of returns with an account holding more than it lost. But then the following 30 days may show a limited volume of growth where a deduction had to be made. Realizing one needs to save and prepare for a period of low income brings with it a knowledge that God is in control. You can find a payment plan will suffice but there will come a day when the ending balance needs to reflect "paid in full". If you harvest and spend with care you will gain a forward momentum in which you preserve your holdings and gain a righteous set of assets. However, if you always spend the revenue to enhance the day of pleasure, you will soon find your losses outweigh your holding assets and you will lose face in a crowd of many. God does not overextend in the way He distributes His grace. He knows what is needed and how much to offer when the need is present. Calculating how to achieve a goal is an aspiration many strive to attain. If you persevere and trust in the operation of management to an expert who has gained notoriety because of fair business dealings, you will grow in the way of good character and so will he. Often there is a dispute as to who the profits should be distributed to and how. A written contract eases the burden and allows for both parties to comprehend their role and responsible integrity will withstand. The courts maintain an eye of revelation when there is a dispute, but God prefers man to negotiate in an orderly manner with integrity.

_____

_____

_____

_____

_____

_____

_____

Today is a preaching where man has made himself above God. He has forgotten the one who gifts and leads. With God the plan will always be right.

A favoring of the Most High grants the mind where to plant and how to make a day's wages benefit the hand. God is a caretaker and a being of intellect in where no other can do as He does. If you lead a group of men but don't truly want to see them succeed, you aren't a good manager nor are you a solid representative of who Christ Jesus is to you. Those who move in a way that prospers many are the ones God will open the door to for more leadership and crafted skills. If you seek fame, build with the thought of being the next capital member who will enact a law that abides with the teaching of true form instead of seeking for your name to be in lights. Fame brings with it a lack of secure holdings as many will desire the glory for themselves as well. A solid character is better than a pocket of gold. A formula to follow is to ask for wealth that leads to a heart where God can maneuver His strength to your person for the benefit of others as well as your own account. God does not respond to those who are after riches for their own enjoyment and no other. This is not the Biblical recognized leadership that is desired by the witness of true love or longevity. You may gain in a way that leads to global recognition but what have you gained if you lose it all to the ones whom you serve. Would it not be better to build for a community in where all parties benefit? Each a direct representative of true understanding that hold to the fact Christ is King and follow the path of true integrity. A shadow of darkness does not lead one to the light. A right turn can escape a catastrophe on the road, but in life it can bring hardship as well as capital employment. Grace is not received unless a heart is pure and ready to entertain the Lord and His call to him personally. Each deployment seen by the hand of God is a character where all who know Him gain intellect and a true order of strength can be felt. If you are weak, open the Word of God and study who Christ is and learn His teachings so you will be prepared to better those around your presence as well as your own inner aspect and clear mental display of a sound commitment to Him personally.

Not all who engage in the power of true acknowledgement toward the King are real in their desire to know who He is as a person. They simply desire to gain a better edge in the way of money making or bounty preserves for their own way forward in life. God knows the true in spirit and He acknowledges the ones who come before Him in faith. The people who truly gain insight have Christ as their purpose in life and He is the Waymaker to their future. They look to him for all their needs, and they expect His presence in their life to balance their inner being. God offers peace and He never fails the mind when it seeks His person. Trust Him and know the rewards He offers are genuine and committed in their wholesomeness.

_____

_____

_____

_____

Closing Words From the Author...

Together working with the Lord, we can build with character. We can enlist one another and form a union where man and God are tied in a reflective manner. All those who trust the leadership God offers, glean a perspective that hold them fast against any wave of hardship. God is not hard to live under nor is He difficult to follow. He has grace and a love that envelop the heart in utter complete hope. With grace at the forefront, man has the opportune employment of a grafted plan that can teach him how to live each day with clear strides and precise endeavors that secure a momentum in the direction of light and a true course of study. Nowhere is there a better guide than the holy Word God offers us freely in scripture. The insight it offers is comparable to no other in any form, written or said. Look at the detail God offers and learn the true way to teach and glean for yourself. I never doubt where my hope comes from. I may fail on occasion in my walk, but God never leaves my side. He will carry all who trust Him to do so. Today I type with closing words to a book I don't know the future of. I simply do as directed and prepare where I am able. I understand my limits and I release my faults and short comings to the great creator. He will handle the details and create a thing of beauty. How this plays out will be determined by His hand alone.

Jesus answered, "I am the way and the truth and the life. No one comes to the Father except through me". John 14:6 NIV

Some History About Robin Arne...

Today Robin Arne replaces moments in time with prayer and reading of the Word of God. She builds with clay and produces written material for many to learn from or hear her insights and thoughts. She is a witness who never forgets where to look for true comfort or hope. She prepares daily by trusting God's direction and gleaning a true connection with His person. She realizes only God can build true character and that His perspective on how to live is what lies at the core of a true witness. Shouldering the responsibility of others is not her work. She is not the hope or true measure of a plan. She simply knows Jesus is the one to follow and she expresses this in her writing material. God is the one to pursue. He is the one to gain insight from and He is the goal Robin sets forth. He never fails her, and she sets her sights toward His person. Today is the opportunity for you to do the same. Trust in scripture and learn the importance of what really matters. You will find faith is the road to a better mental outlook and you will improve your thought process when you apply it toward Jesus alone. Thinking about the future may cause alarm but remember Christ never forgets His people. Build in faith and step toward hope in the way of listening for the spirit of God to direct your path. Trust builds a witness, and you will represent a plan of measure worthy of opportune investment that will gift you with real incentive. Robin will reflect on days like this, and she will attest to the strength God offers her in the form of knowledge or wisdom. Her character is built upon but always growing. The walk is stable but never ending. You can find her reading or incorporating the principles she has gleaned by way of the Master's hand. She holds the Bible as gospel and doesn't doubt its value. The Waymaker has provided much, and she respects His decision making. Hers alone holds no value but with Christ she builds with character and goals of beauty unfold. Today never ends as each moment in time represents this hour at its finest. Learn to embrace the object of purity by holding fast to the Savior. This is a pattern which brings fruit of everlasting longevity. You will find comfort from the King when you entertain His person.

Trust this measure and do well. His promises are real, and a sturdy measure of hope is on every page of His Word, and they are crafted with care.

Robin Arne is available for author interviews. For more information contact us at info@advbooks.com

To purchase additional copies of these books, visit our bookstore at www.advbookstore.com